APPLIED ECONOMICS

BY THE SAME AUTHOR

Basic Economics: A Citizen's Guide to the Economy
Classical Economics Reconsidered
Knowledge and Decisions
Marxism: Philosophy and Economics
Say's Law

APPLIED ECONOMICS

Thinking Beyond Stage One

THOMAS SOWELL

BASIC
BOOKS

A Member of the Perseus Books Group
New York

Copyright © 2004 by Thomas Sowell
Published by Basic Books,
A Member of the Perseus Books Group

Books published by Basic Books are available at special discounts for bulk purchases in the United States by corporations, institutions, and other organizations. For more information, please contact the Special Markets Department at the Perseus Books Group, 11 Cambridge Center, Cambridge MA 02142, or call (617) 252-5298, (800) 255-1514 or e-mail j.mccrary@perseusbooks.com.

Set in 12-point Adobe Caslon by the Perseus Books Group

Library of Congress Cataloging-in-Publication Data

Sowell, Thomas, 1930-
  Applied economics : thinking beyond stage one / Thomas Sowell
    p. cm.
  Includes bibliographical references and index.
  ISBN-13 978-0-465-08143-1   ISBN-10 0-465-08143-6
  1. Economics—Political aspects. 2. Economic policy—Social aspects. 3. Equality.
4. Social problems. 5. Economic development. 6. Economics. I. Title.

HB74.P65S66 2003
330—dc21

                                                          2003010562

DHSB   10 9

To Professor Arthur Smithies,

who taught me to think beyond stage one

CONTENTS

PREFACE

It is one thing to know the basic principles of economics. It is another to apply them to the problems of the real world. Yet that is ultimately what these principles are all about. Instead of focussing on establishing the principles of economics, as I did in *Basic Economics*, here the focus will be on dealing in depth with particular real world problems, using economic principles to clarify why and how things have happened the way that they have. This is a book to enable the general reader, with no prior knowledge of economics, to understand some of the key economic issues of our time— medical care, housing, discrimination, and the economic development of nations, for example. Because these are political, as well as economic issues, some political principles will need to be considered as well. That is, we will need to consider what incentives and constraints apply to political decision-making, as well as those which apply to economic decisions-making.

Neither economics nor politics is just a matter of opinion and both require thinking beyond the immediate consequences of decisions to their long-term effects. Because so few politicians look beyond the next election, it is all the more important that the voters look ahead.

It is helpful to have something of a sense of humor when considering economic policies. Otherwise, the study of these policies and their often painful unintended consequences can get to be too depressing or you can get too angry. Save your anger until you are in the voting booth on election day. In the meantime, enjoy the process of getting more understanding of issues and institutions that affect your life and the future of the country.

Because this is a book for the general public, the usual footnotes or endnotes are omitted. However, for those readers who want to verify what is said here, or to read further on some of the subjects covered, the sources of the many facts discussed here are listed in the back of the book.

THOMAS SOWELL
The Hoover Institution
Stanford University

Chapter 1

Politics versus Economics

When we are talking about applied economic policies, we are no longer talking about pure economic principles, but about the interactions of politics and economics. The principles of economics remain the same, but the likelihood of those principles being applied unchanged is considerably reduced, because politics has its own principles and imperatives. It is not just that politicians' top priority is getting elected and re-elected, or that their time horizon seldom extends beyond the next election. The general public as well behaves differently when making political decisions rather than economic decisions. Virtually no one puts as much time and close attention into deciding whether to vote for one candidate rather than another as is usually put into deciding whether to buy one house rather than another—or perhaps even one car rather than another.

The voter's political decisions involve having a minute influence on policies which affect many other people, while economic decision-making is about having a major effect on one's own personal well-being. It should not be surprising that the quantity and quality of thinking going into these very different kinds of decisions differ correspondingly. One of the ways in which these decisions differ is in not thinking through political decisions beyond the immediate consequences. When most voters do not think beyond stage one, many elected officials have no incentive to weigh what the consequences will be in later stages—and considerable incentives to avoid getting beyond what their constituents think and understand, for fear that rival politicians can drive a wedge between them and their constituents by catering to public misconceptions.

The very way that issues are conceived tends to be different in politics and in economics. Political thinking tends to conceive of policies, institutions, or programs in terms of their *hoped-for results*—"drug prevention" programs, "profit-making" enterprises, "public-interest" law firms, "gun control" laws, and so forth. But for purposes of economic analysis, what matters is not what goals are being sought but what incentives and constraints are being created in pursuit of those goals. We know, for example, that many—if not most—"profit-making" enterprises do not in fact make profits, as shown by the high percentage of new businesses that go out of business within a few years after being created. Similarly, it is an open question whether drug prevention programs actually prevent or reduce drug usage, whether public interest law firms actually benefit the public, or whether gun control laws actually control guns. No economist is likely to be surprised when rent control laws, for example, lead to housing shortages and fail to control rent, so that cities with such laws often end up with higher rents than cities without them. But such outcomes may be very surprising to people who think in terms of political rhetoric focussed on desirable goals.

The point is not simply that various policies may fail to achieve their purposes. The more fundamental point is that we need to know the *actual characteristics* of the processes set in motion—and the incentives and constraints inherent in such characteristics—rather than judging these processes by their goals. Many of the "unintended consequences" of policies and programs would have

been foreseeable from the outset if these processes had been analyzed in terms of the incentives and constraints they created, instead of in terms of the desirability of the goals they proclaimed.
Once we start thinking in terms of the chain of events set in motion by particular policies—and following these events beyond
stage one—the world begins to look very different.

Politics and the market are both ways of getting some people to
respond to other people's desires. Consumers choosing which
goods to spend their money on have often been analogized to
voters deciding which candidates to elect to public office. However, the two processes are profoundly different. Not only do
individuals invest very different amounts of time and thought in
making economic versus political decisions, those decisions are
inherently different in themselves. Voters decide *whether* to vote
for one candidate or another but they decide *how much* of what
kinds of food, clothing, shelter, etc., to purchase. In short, political decisions tend to be categorical, while economic decisions
tend to be incremental.

Incremental decisions can be more fine-tuned than deciding
which candidate's whole package of principles and practices comes
closest to meeting your own desires. Incremental decision-making
also means that not every increment of even very desirable things is
likewise necessarily desirable, given that there are other things that
the money could be spent on after having acquired a given amount
of a particular good or service. For example, although it might be
worthwhile spending considerable money to live in a nice home,
buying a second home in the country may or may not be worth
spending money that could be used for sending a child to college or
for recreational travel overseas. One consequence of incremental decision-making is that increments of many desirable things remain
unpurchased because they are almost—but not quite—worth the
sacrifices required to get them.

From a political standpoint, this means that there are always numerous desirable things that government officials can offer to provide to voters who want them—either free of charge or at reduced, government-subsidized prices—even when these voters do not want these increments enough to sacrifice their own money to pay for them. Ultimately, of course, the public ends up paying as taxpayers for things that they would not have chosen to pay for as consumers. The real winners in this process are the politicians whose apparent generosity and compassion gain them political support.

In trying to understand the effect of politics on economics, we need to consider not only officials' responses to the various pressures they receive from different sources, but also the way that the media and the voting public see economic issues. Both the media and the voters are prone to what might be called one-stage thinking.

ONE-STAGE THINKING

When I was an undergraduate studying economics under Professor Arthur Smithies of Harvard, he asked me in class one day what policy I favored on a particular issue of the times. Since I had strong feelings on that issue, I proceeded to answer him with enthusiasm, explaining what beneficial consequences I expected from the policy I advocated.

"And then what will happen?" he asked.

The question caught me off guard. However, as I thought about it, it became clear that the situation I described would lead to other economic consequences, which I then began to consider and to spell out.

"And what will happen after that?" Professor Smithies asked.

As I analyzed how the further economic reactions to the policy would unfold, I began to realize that these reactions would lead to consequences much less desirable than those at the first stage, and I began to waver somewhat.

"And *then* what will happen?" Smithies persisted.

By now I was beginning to see that the economic reverberations of the policy I advocated were likely to be pretty disastrous—and, in fact, much worse than the initial situation that it was designed to improve.

Simple as this little exercise may sound, it goes further than most economic discussions about policies on a wide range of issues. Most thinking stops at stage one. In recent years, former economic advisers to presidents of the United States—from both political parties—have commented publicly on how little thinking ahead about economic consequences went into decisions made at the highest level.[1] This is not to say that there was no thinking ahead about *political* consequences. Each of the presidents they served (Nixon and Clinton) was so successful politically that he was re-elected by a wider margin than the vote that first put him in office.

Incentives and Consequences

Thinking beyond stage one is especially important when considering policies whose consequences unfold over a period of years. If the initial consequences are good, and the bad consequences come later—especially if later is after the next election—then it is always tempting for politicians to adopt such policies.

---

[1] Herbert Stein and Joseph Stiglitz.

For example, if a given city or state contains a number of prosperous corporations, nothing is easier than to raise money to finance local government projects that will win votes for their sponsors by raising the tax rates on these corporations. What are the corporations going to do? Pick up their factories, hotels, railroads, or office buildings and move somewhere else? Certainly not immediately, in stage one. Even if they could sell their local properties and go buy replacements somewhere else, this would take time and not all their experienced employees would be willing to move suddenly with them to another city or state. Nevertheless, even under such restrictions on movement, the high taxes would begin to have some immediate effect.

Businesses are always going out of business and being replaced by new businesses that arise. In high-tax cities and states, there is likely to be an increase in the rate at which businesses go out of business, as some struggling firms that might have been able to hold on longer, and perhaps ride out their problems, are unable to do so when heavy tax burdens are added to their other problems. Meanwhile, newly arising companies have options when deciding where to locate their factories or offices, and cities and states with high tax rates are likely to be avoided. Therefore, even if all existing and thriving corporations are unable to budge in the short run, the high-tax jurisdictions can begin the process of losing businesses, even in stage one. But the losses may not be on a scale that is large enough to be noticeable.

Then comes stage two. Usually the headquarters where a business' top brass work can be moved before the operating units that have larger numbers of employees and much equipment. Moreover, if the corporation has other operating units in other cities and states—or perhaps overseas—it can begin shifting some of its production to other locations, where taxes are not so high, even if it does not immediately abandon its factories or offices at given sites. This reduction in the amount of business done locally in the high-tax location will in turn begin to reduce the locally earned income on which taxes are paid by both the corporation and its local employees.

Stage three: As corporations grow over time, they can choose to locate their new operations where taxes are not so high, transferring employees who are willing to move and replacing those who are not by hiring new people. Stage four: As more and more corporations desert the high-tax city or state, eventually the point can be reached where the total tax revenues collected from corporations under higher tax rates are less than what was collected under the lower rates of the past, when there were more businesses paying those taxes. By this time, however, years may have passed and the politicians responsible for setting this process in motion may well have moved on to higher office in state or national government.

More important, even those politicians who remain in office in the local area are unlikely to be blamed for declining tax revenues, lost employment, or cutbacks in government services and neglected infrastructure made necessary by an inadequate tax base. In short, those responsible for such economic declines will probably escape political consequences, unless either the voters or the media think beyond stage one and follow the sequence of events over a period of years—which seldom happens.[2]

---

[2]There is another sense in which multiple stages must be taken into account, which may be easier to explain by analogy. Imagine that a dam can be emptied into a valley and that calculations show that this would fill the valley with water to a depth of 20 feet. If your home is located on an elevation 30 feet above the valley floor, it should be safe if the water is slowly released. But if the floodgates are simply flung wide open, a wave of water 40 feet high may roar across the valley, smashing your home and drowning everyone in it. After the water subsides, it will still end up just 20 feet deep, but that will not matter as far as the destruction of the home and people are concerned, even though both are now 10 feet above the level at which the water settles down. A Nobel Prize–winning economist has argued that economic policies suddenly imposed on various Third World countries by the International Monetary Fund have ignored the timing and sequence of reactions inside those countries, which may include irreparable damage to the social fabric as economic desperation creates mass riots that can topple governments and make foreign investors unwilling to put money into such an unstable country for years to come.

New York City has been a classic example of this process. Once the headquarters of many of the biggest corporations in America, New York in the early twenty-first century was headquarters to just one of the 100 fastest growing companies in the country. With the highest tax rate of any American city and the highest real estate tax per square foot of business office space, New York has been losing businesses and hundreds of thousands of jobs. Meanwhile, the city has been spending twice as much per capita as Los Angeles and three times as much per capita as Chicago on a wide variety of municipal programs. By and large, spend-and-tax policies have been successful politically, however negative their economic consequences.

In short, killing the goose that lays the golden egg is a viable political strategy, so long as the goose does not die before the next election and no one traces the politicians' fingerprints on the murder weapon. Looking at it in another sense, when you have agents or surrogates looking out for your interests, in any aspect of life—political or otherwise—there is always the danger that they will look out for their own interests, which do not always coincide with yours. Corporate managements do not always put the stockholders' interest first, and agents for actors, athletes, or writers may sacrifice their clients' interests to their own. There is no reason to expect elected officials to be fundamentally different. But there are reasons to know what their incentives are—and what the economic realities are that they may overlook while pursuing their own political goals.

Such one-stage thinking is not peculiar to the United States or to tax issues. On the other side of the world, an Indian writer observed the same phenomenon as regards education reform:

No one bothers about education because results take a long time to come. When a politician promises rice for two rupees (12 cents a pound) when it costs five rupees in the market (31 cents a pound), he wins the election. N. T. Rama Rao did precisely that in the 1994 state elections. He won the election, became the chief minister, and nearly bankrupted the state treasury. He also sent a sobering message to Prime Minister Narasimha Rao in Delhi, who, according to some observers, slowed India's reforms because he realized that votes resided in populist measures and not in doing what is right for the long run. Since the 1980s politicians have competed in giving away free goods and services to voters. When politicians do that, where is the money to come from for creating new schools or improving old ones?

I became thoroughly depressed the day the Punjab chief minister, Prakash Singh Badal, gave away free electricity and water to farmers in February 1997. He had lived up to his electoral promises, but twelve months later the state's fragile finances were destroyed and there was no money to pay salaries to civil servants.

Like taxes, subsidies also have further repercussions that can make the country as a whole worse off, even when the subsidies are not paid for out of the government's treasury but are created by having one good or service subsidize another. Subsidized train fare in India, for example, are paid for by raising freight charges. No doubt this wins more votes among passengers than the votes lost among shippers, simply because there are likely to be far more passengers. However, the economic result of these artificially high freight charges, according to the distinguished British magazine *The Economist*, is that "power plants in the south of India find it cheaper to import coal from Australia than to buy it from Bihar." Meanwhile, Bihar is one of the poorest states in India and could very much use additional jobs in its coal industry.

Even when dealing with emergency situations, public officials may think of themselves and their own political needs before they think of the victims and their plight. According to Indian econo-mist Barun Mitra: "The super cyclone that hit the coasts of eastern Indian state of Orissa in November 1999, left more than 10,000 people officially dead. But unofficial reports continued to put the figure at more than double that number. There were reports in the media that the Central Government in Delhi was reluctant to seek international help, because this in some way might be a reflection on the competence of the national government. And this despite the fact that even two weeks after the tragedy, many villages re-mained cut-off without any information coming or relief reaching the survivors."

What about the reaction of a market economy to such a disaster? Few insurance companies could drag their feet like this and expect to survive in a competitive economy, because people would switch to buying the policies of some rival insurance company. But most government agencies are monopolies. If you don't like the slow re-sponse of a government emergency relief agency, there is no rival government emergency relief agency that you can turn to instead. Monopoly tends toward self-indulgent inefficiency, whether it is a private monopoly or a government monopoly. The difference is that monopoly is the norm for government agencies, while few private businesses are able to prevent rival firms from arising to challenge them for customers.

Those who think no further than stage one often regard the gov-ernment's power to control prices as a way of reducing the costs of various goods and service, thus making them more widely afford-able. Such policies as "bringing down the cost of prescription drugs" or making housing "affordable" often seem very attractive when thinking no further than stage one. However, even in stage one, there is a fundamental difference between truly bringing down the costs of particular goods and services and simply forbid-ding prices from reflecting those costs.

A classic example of controlling prices without controlling costs was the electricity crisis in California in 2001 and 2002. The costs of generating the electricity used by Californians rose substantially for a number of reasons. Reduced rainfall on the west coast meant reduced water flow through hydroelectric dams and consequently less electricity was generated there. Since the costs of running these dams did not fall correspondingly, this meant that the cost of generating a given amount of electricity rose. At the same time, the costs of such fuels as oil and natural gas were also rising, so that the costs of generating electricity in these ways was also increasing. In the normal course of events, such rising costs would have been reflected in higher prices on California consumers' electric bills, which would provide incentives for those consumers to reduce their use of electricity. But California politicians came to their rescue by imposing legal limits on how high electricity prices would be permitted to rise. That was stage one.

While those who generated electricity passed on their costs when they sold the electricity wholesale to the public utility companies, which directly supplied the public, these public utilities were forbidden to charge the public more than the legally prescribed price. Thus when wholesale electricity prices were 15 cents per kilowatt hour, the retail price remained at 7 cents per kilowatt hour. As an economic study of the industry put it:

> Wholesale prices signaled that electricity was increasingly scarce, but retail prices told consumers that nothing had changed. Accordingly, consumers demanded more electricity than was available.

Blackouts were the inevitable result. That was stage two.

Stage three saw California politicians scrambling to find some way to stop the blackouts, which not only disrupted homes and businesses currently, but threatened to drive some businesses out of the state, which would deprive California of both jobs and taxes. Worse yet, from the politicians' perspective, it threatened their re-election prospects. Stage four saw California public utility companies going bankrupt, as they bought electricity from wholesalers at higher prices than they were allowed to charge their customers. The public utilities' lack of money and declining credit ratings then led the wholesalers to refuse to continue supplying them with electricity. Things were now truly desperate, so the governor stepped in and used the state's money to buy the electricity that the wholesalers would not sell to the financially strapped utility companies on credit.

In the end, Californians paid more for their electricity—only partly on their electric bills and the rest on their tax bills or in reduced government services as the state's record budget surplus turned into a record deficit. It is doubtful whether Californians paid a dime less after the politicians' grandstand rescue of them with price controls than they would have paid had the state government stayed out of it and let the price be determined by supply and demand. When all the costs are counted, they may well have ended up paying more than they would have if the increased costs had simply led to higher prices through the marketplace. But the governor was re-elected.

In general outlines, none of this was unique to California or to electricity. Price controls have been causing shortages in countries around the world, and for literally thousands of years of recorded history, whether the prices that were being controlled were the prices of food, housing, fuel, medical care, or innumerable other goods and services. Almost all these price controls were popular when they were first instituted because most people did not think beyond stage one. After imposing the first peacetime wage and price controls in American history, President Richard Nixon was re-elected in a landslide, even though he had been elected initially by a very narrow margin.

Another major difference between private and governmental institutions is that, no matter how big and successful a private business is, it can always be forced out of business when it is no longer satisfying its customers—whether because of its own inadequacies or because competing firms or alternative technologies can satisfy the customers better. Government agencies, however, can continue on despite demonstrable failures, and the power of government can prevent rivals from arising.

Despite innumerable complaints about the U. S. Postal Service over the years, it continues to maintain a monopoly so strict that it is illegal for anyone else to put things in a citizen's mailbox, even though that mailbox was bought and paid for by the citizen, rather than by the government. Postal authorities clearly understand what a competitive threat it would be to them if the public had a choice of private companies delivering mail to their homes. Private package-delivery companies like United Parcel Service and Federal Express have long ago overtaken the Postal Service in the number of packages delivered. Indeed, federal government agencies themselves often prefer to rely on private package-delivery companies.

Recycling

Prices play many roles in allocating time and effort, as well as goods and services. Recycling, for example, requires time and effort, and the incremental value of the things being recycled may or may not be worth the time and effort spent in salvaging them. Where the incremental value of the salvaged goods is greater than the value of the alternative uses of the time and effort, recycling can take place spontaneously, as a result of the ordinary operations of a free market—without laws or exhortations. There are some salvageable things whose incremental value would lead to their being recycled without government intervention and other salvageable things whose incremental value would lead to their being thrown away. Recycling is not categorically justified or unjustified, but is incrementally either worth or not worth the costs.

In some Third World countries, or among the chronically unemployed or homeless population in affluent countries like the United States, it may make perfect sense to collect discarded cans and bottles to sell—and some people do so voluntarily, without being forced or exhorted to do so. In mid-twentieth century West Africa, a distinguished British economist named Peter Bauer noted the "extensive trade in empty containers such as kerosene, cigarette and soup tins, flour, salt, and cement bags and beer bottles." Although many third-party European observers at that time regarded such African recycling activities as wasteful uses of labor because Europeans did not spend their time doing such things, Professor Bauer explained why it was not wasteful:

> Some types of container are turned into various household articles or other commodities. Cigarette and soup tins become small oil lamps, and salt bags are made into shirts or tunics. But more usually the containers are used again in the storage and movement of goods. Those who seek out, purchase, and carry and distribute second-hand containers maintain the stock of capital. They prevent the destruction of the containers, usually improve their condition, distribute them to where they can best be used, and so extend their usefulness, the intensity of their use, and their effective life. The activities of the traders represent a substitution of labour for capital.

Most of these African recyclers were women and children, and the meager alternative employment open to them made it efficient for them to make a small profit on recycled containers, when that profit exceeded what they could earn elsewhere. It was also more efficient for the society as a whole: "So far from the system being wasteful it is highly economic in substituting superabundant for scarce resources"—the superabundant resource being the time of otherwise idle labor.

Both when recycling was criticized in mid-twentieth century Africa and exhorted in late-twentieth century America, third-party observers simply assumed that they had superior understanding than that of the people directly involved, even though these observers had seldom bothered to think through the economics of what they were saying. At some point it pays virtually everyone to recycle and at some other point it pays virtually no one. What is crucial is the value of the thing being recycled and the value of the alternative uses of resources, including the time of the people who might do the recycling.

Even in an affluent country such as the United States, cameras have long been recycled, and there are stores such as KEH in Atlanta or Midwest Photo in Columbus which specialize in nationwide sales of used cameras, most costing hundreds of dollars each and some costing thousands. The sale of used cars has likewise long been common virtually everywhere, and most houses that are sold are used houses, though that term is almost never applied, because houses that have been lived in before are the norm, even among mansions, and it is newly built houses which are singled out for labeling.

Where recycling takes place only in response to political pressures and exhortations, it need not meet the test of being incrementally worth its incremental costs. Accordingly, studies of government-imposed recycling programs in the United States have shown that what they salvage is usually worth less than the cost of salvaging it. This situation is parallel with inducing people to pay as taxpayers for incremental benefits that they would not pay for as consumers.

CENTRAL PLANNING VERSUS MARKETS

Differences between political decision-making and economic decision-making stand out in sharpest contrast when comparing whole systems of comprehensive economic planning by government officials with economic systems in which market competition among privately owned businesses determines what is produced by whom and at what prices. In both cases—socialism[3] and capitalism—the rationales of the systems must be compared with the actual results, the rhetoric with the reality. The relevant question is not which system sounds more plausible but which produces what results.

What must also be understood is that both systems—in fact, all economic systems, including feudalism, fascism and voluntary collectives—operate within the inherent constraint that what everyone wants adds up to more than they can possibly get. This means that all economic systems must find ways of restricting and denying the use of both resources and finished products through one mechanism or another. In some systems this is done by imposing rationing or central allocation and in other systems people ration themselves according to how much money they have available to spend for various items.

All economic systems not only provide people with goods and services, but also restrict or prevent them from getting as much of these goods and services as they wish, since no economy can supply everything that everyone wants in the amounts that everyone wants. The systems differ in the manner in which they restrict

---

[3]While socialism may be conceived of in political terms as a system that aims at greater equality, a planned economy, job security, and other humane goals, in economic terms socialism is more likely to be described in terms of what it actually does, rather than in terms of what it hopes to achieve. In these latter terms, socialism is a system in which property rights in industry, commerce, and agriculture can be defined and assigned only by political authorities, rather than by private transactions among individuals and organizations in the marketplace. Whether such arrangements actually lead toward or away from the various proclaimed goals of socialism is left as an empirical question, rather than a foregone conclusion.

consumption and in the effectiveness with which they allocate resources in ways that produce lower or higher standards of living.

Central Planning

The term "planning" is often used to describe an economic system where the key decisions are made by political authorities, whether these are democratically elected officials or representatives of a communist or other totalitarian government. However, there is just as much planning engaged in by owners and managers of private enterprises under capitalism. The difference is in who is planning for whom. In a free market economy, millions of consumers, business owners and managers, investors, and others have their own plans—each for his or her own well-being, leaving the overall coordination of these plans in the economy at large to changing prices and the economic incentives that these prices provide for mutual accommodation. What has generally been called "planning" has been *central* planning—planning by a small group of officials for the economy as a whole.

The same general principle of collective decision-making has also been applied by smaller settlements, such as the Israeli kibbutz[4] or various other small enclaves of like-minded people who wish to produce and consume collectively, outside the framework of a capitalist market economy.

The most thorough-going control of entire national economies occurred during the era of the Soviet Union, which set a pattern that was later followed in China and other communist states. However, the governments of India and France also at one time

---

[4]There are many forms of socialism, including the voluntary socialism of the kibbutz in Israel, as distinguished from the state-imposed socialism of the Soviet Union or Maoist China. So devoted to ideals of equality and sharing were the members of the kibbutz that there were objections when one young member received a gift of a teapot from her parents, who lived outside the kibbutz, and she "began to brew tea in her own room, and to invite some friends to join her." Purists "regarded the

either owned or controlled large segments of their respective economies. Moreover, wide sections of the political, intellectual and even business communities were often in favor of this expansive role of government. Swedish economist Gunnar Myrdal defined economic central planning this way:

> The basic idea of economic planning is that the state shall take an active, indeed the decisive, role in the economy: by its own acts of enterprise and investment, and by its various controls—inducements and restrictions—over the private sector, the state shall initiate, spur, and steer economic development. These public policy measures shall be coordinated and the coordination made explicit in an over-all plan for a specified number of years ahead.

Although some have contrasted government planning with uncontrolled chaos in the private marketplace, in fact government central planning means *over-riding other people's plans*, since private individuals and organizations have their own plans, which are coordinated with one another through price movements. How well either set of plans is likely to work out is the issue. For much of the twentieth century, it was widely assumed that central planning was more likely to produce desired results than the uncontrolled competition of the marketplace. It was only after such planning was put into effect in a variety of countries around the world that the results turned out to be worse than anyone expected—leaving planned economies falling behind the economic progress in countries where the coordination of the economy as a whole was left to market competition and resulting price movements that directed

---

possession of a private teapot not only as a breach of equality but also as an egregious violation of the principle of communal eating and an unacceptable rejection of communality in favor of personal privacy. It symbolized the erosion of society by a gradual accommodation to the baser human drives, and the 'teapot scandal' as it became known, was debated endlessly in the General Meetings throughout the kibbutz movement."

resources and products to where they were most in demand. By the last decade of the twentieth century, even socialist governments and communist governments had begun abandoning central planning and selling government-owned enterprises to private entrepreneurs.

Prices not only direct goods and the resources needed to produce goods where they are most in demand, these prices also force consumers to limit their own consumption. Just as we can appreciate the important role of water more clearly during a drought, so the role of prices can be more clearly demonstrated by looking at places where prices are not allowed to play their usual role. For example, communal living in a kibbutz in Israel was based on its members' collectively producing and supplying their members' needs, without resort to money or prices. However, supplying electricity and food without charging prices led to a situation where electric lights were left on during the day, and members would bring friends from outside the kibbutz to join them for meals. Later, after the kibbutz began to charge prices for electricity and food, there was a sharp drop in the consumption of both.

The presence or absence of prices affects the use of the resources which go into the production of goods, as well as in the consumption of the goods themselves. Soviet industry used more electricity than American industry, even though American industry produced more output. Enterprises in the United States had to pay market prices for electricity and keep their production costs below the prices that supply and demand in the market would allow them to charge for their output. Otherwise they would make losses and face the risk of bankruptcy. Soviet enterprises faced no such incentives or constraints. Nor was electricity unique. More material inputs and energy in general went into producing a given amount of output in the Union of Soviet Socialist Republics than was used to produce the same output in the United States, Germany or Japan.

The USSR had one of the richest endowments of natural resources on earth, including more petroleum deposits than any other country outside of the Middle East, and some of the most fertile farmland on the continent of Europe. Moreover, the Soviet Union had a well-educated population, including many scientists, engineers, and technicians. But, while it seemed to have all the ingredients of national prosperity, it was in fact much poorer than the United States or the countries of western Europe. What was missing in its economy were the incentives and mechanisms capable of converting its abundant inputs into output at a rate comparable to that of the United States or other countries with price-coordinated markets.

Although the USSR had prices, these were prices set by central planners, and did not reflect the relative scarcities of particular resources, as prices resulting from supply and demand in competitive markets tend to do. Nor was it clear how centrally planned prices could have reflected anything so complex and volatile as the ever changing relative scarcities of innumerable resources and finished products, since there were 20 million prices for central planners to set.

This was a virtually impossible task for the central planners to perform well, though it presents no special problem in a market economy where millions of consumers and producers each keep track of, and influence, a relative handful of prices which directly affect them.[5] The net result was that it was common for the Soviet Union to have warehouses bulging with unwanted and unsold goods, while people were lined up in queues for other things that

---

[5]Most of us, if not all of us, are utterly ignorant of the prices of well over 90 percent of the things produced in our economy. Do you know the price of a Harley-Davidson motorcycle or a Linhof camera or an appendix operation at your local hospital?

they wanted and hoped to get before supplies ran out. A visitor to the Soviet Union in 1987 reported, "long lines of people still stood patiently for hours to buy things: on one street corner people were waiting to buy tomatoes from a cardboard box, one to a customer, and outside a shop next to our hotel there was a line for three days, about which we learned that on the day of our arrival that shop had received a new shipment of men's undershirts."

In a capitalist economy, the prices of the surplus goods piled up in warehouses would have fallen because of supply and demand, forcing the enterprises which produced them to cut back production, in order to avoid continuing losses. This in turn would release resources (including labor) that would be in demand in other sectors of the economy, where shortages and rising prices would have produced higher profits—and thus greater demand for the labor and raw materials needed to increase the supply of the more profitable output. But no such process took place in a socialist economy, where simultaneous shortages and surpluses could persist for years, until overburdened central planners could get around to dealing with each problem.

Hiring more central planners would not solve the problem, which was that millions of prices had to be adjusted *relative to one another*, so you could not put one group of central planners in charge of setting prices for furs and another in charge of setting prices for undershirts, because the whole point was that too many resources had been devoted to producing animal pelts that were rotting in warehouses while people had trouble finding enough undershirts.

None of this was peculiar to the Soviet Union. Similar problems dogged other centrally planned societies, whether democratic societies like India or totalitarian countries like China. The USSR was a particularly striking example of the problems of central planning because it was a country richly endowed with a wide range of natural resources, whose people were nevertheless poor. Japan and Switzerland are contrary examples of capitalist countries with meager natural resources which nevertheless have some of the highest standards of living in the world. The peoples of the Soviet Union paid a high price for central planning. As a book by two Soviet economists pointed out, "not until the 1950s were we able to exceed the 1913 per capita level of agricultural output" and—writing in the late 1980s—per capita meat consumption "remains lower than it was in 1927."

China, after the death of Mao Zedong, began a piecemeal conversion from central planning to free markets—first in very limited geographical areas, and then expanded the operation of markets as those areas began to prosper dramatically more so than other parts of the country. As markets replaced politically managed economic decision-making, China experienced one of the highest economic growth rates in the world.

Although India had more than double the Gross National Income per capita of China in 1970, China had nearly caught up by 1991 and by 2000 had nearly double the Gross National Income per capita of India. Belatedly, India too began to rid itself of many government directives and controls and "freed the country's entrepreneurs for the first time since independence" in 1947, in the words of the London magazine *The Economist*. There followed a new growth rate of 6 percent a year, making India "one of the world's fastest-growing big economies."

Despite the sharp distinction in principle between government-planned economies and market economies, in reality there is a continuum between the two. Even in the days of the Soviet Union under Josef Stalin's iron control, some minor elements of free market activity were permitted, such as allowing people to sell produce grown on small plots of land around their homes. These gardens, incidentally, turned out to supply nearly a third of the agricultural output in the USSR, even though they occupied a tiny fraction of the land. Meanwhile, no capitalist country has ever been 100 percent free of government controls and directives. Just as Soviet agriculture was not 100 percent government-controlled, so American agriculture is not 100 percent free of government controls. Nor is American industry.

Price-Coordinated Economies

There are many names for economies in which individual plans and actions are coordinated by price movements in response to supply and demand, which serve as incentives for the different individuals to accommodate their respective plans to the total resources available. These terms include capitalism and the free market. But what such economies actually do, regardless of what they are called, is depend upon price movements to move resources, finished products, and people themselves to where they are in demand, without any central authority trying to control the whole process. This process may sound implausible to those who have never lived in such an economy, and even to some of those who have. One small but revealing episode involved the last Soviet premier, Mikhail Gorbachev, asking British Prime Minister Margaret Thatcher: How do you see to it that people get food? The answer was that she didn't. Prices did that. Yet the British people were better fed than those in the Soviet Union, even though the British have not grown enough food to feed themselves in more than a century. Prices bring them food from other countries.

Considering what a monumental task it is to supply tons of food every day to a city the size of London or New York, it is remarkable that we take it for granted that such a task is performed without anyone's being in charge of seeing that it all gets done. It would be remarkable even if Londoners or New Yorkers were supplied with only some very basic things to eat like bread and milk. In reality, they are supplied with an incredible range of fresh, frozen, canned, dried, organic, Chinese, Italian, Mexican, French, Vietnamese, and other foods every day—all with no overall plan or control, except by prices responding to ever-changing supply and demand. No given individual, either in or out of government, even knows how much of all these things are brought into the city while it is happening, and often there are only estimates after the fact.

The operation of a free market may not even sound plausible, but it works, while the idea of a "planned economy" has sounded both plausible and attractive to many of the best educated people in the world, until it was demonstrated, again and again, in innumerable countries and at painful costs, that it does not work.

Failure is a big part of a free market's success. People fail to live up to their potential, or to carry out all their good intentions, in all kinds of economic and political systems. Capitalism makes them pay a price for their failures, while socialism, feudalism, fascism and other systems enable personal failures, especially by those at the top, to be ignored and the inevitable price to be paid by others in lower standards of living than they could have had with the existing resources and technology. There was a reason why long-time Soviet dictator Josef Stalin kept a tight rein on what Soviet citizens could learn about the west, severely restricting travel and blocking most western writings or broadcasts from entering the USSR.

At one time, however, the Soviet authorities thought that it would be a propaganda coup to show their people an American television program about the plight of blacks in the United States. But this plan backfired when what most struck the Soviet viewers was the obviously higher standard of living that American blacks had, compared to the standard of living in the USSR.[6]

The economic advantages of a market economy are accompanied by political disadvantages. Its over-all operations are seldom understood, even by those who are successful at running their own individual businesses, and their articulation seldom matches that of intellectuals, who usually have neither experience in business nor expertise in economics. More fundamentally, the main incentive of capitalism is self-interest, which is by no means an attractive quality, however effective it may be for producing economic results—for others as well as for oneself.

The very expression "the market" suggests something impersonal, when in fact what is involved are simply all the very personal individual choices which are reconciled with one another through the competitive processes which are summarized as "the market." When a newspaper headline asks, "Should the Internet be Left to the Market," what this question really amounts to is: Should individuals be free to use the Internet as they wish or should some collective body restrict or direct what they do? A case can be made for or against restrictions on using the Internet, but that is the real issue.

Alternatives to a market economy may express nobler sentiments but the bottom line is whether this in fact leads to better behavior in terms of better serving their fellow human beings.

For example, a conscientious Soviet worker who was loading bread began to notice that the bread had bird droppings on it. She returned it to the bakery but was later told by a driver that this bread was not thrown out. It was simply ground up with the flour used to bake fresh bread and the finished product was then deliv-

---

[6]When I saw the apartment buildings that Russians were living in, in St. Petersburg, the first thought that occurred to me was that I had seen better buildings than this boarded up in the poverty-stricken South Bronx.

ered to the stores, with the bird droppings now on the inside instead of on the outside. A capitalist enterprise doing such a thing would not only be liable to lawsuits and prosecution, it would risk losing its customers to its competitors if word ever got out, and could be ruined economically even before legal processes ran their course. But a government monopoly has less to fear. Environmental degradation was likewise worse in the Communist bloc in Eastern Europe than in capitalist countries, and the worst environmental disaster of all occurred in the Soviet Union at the Chernobyl nuclear power plant. Moreover, the ability of a totalitarian government to keep information secret meant that local Soviet officials could evacuate their own families first, while leaving the local population wholly uninformed and exposed to thousands of times more radiation than normal. Only after foreign countries detected the increased radiation in their own atmospheres and foreign radio broadcasts then began reaching the Soviet Union did ordinary people in the contaminated area learn that they were in danger.

IMPLICATIONS

To contrast the making of economic and social decisions through politics and through the market is not to say that no other social processes can deal with such activities or issues. Obviously families, philanthropy, cooperative, and volunteer organizations and numerous other institutions and arrangements can affect and influence many of the same things that markets and governments handle.

Even the staunchest free market economists may, in their own families, follow principles very much like the old socialist doctrine of "from each according to his ability, to each according to his needs." Thus a child who has contributed little or nothing to the family's economic resources may absorb growing amounts of those resources over the years, especially when being supported for four or more years in college. Informal arrangements have many advantages over both markets and governments but different things can be better handled by a variety of social processes.[7] The persistence for centuries of both governments and market economies strongly suggests that each fills a vital role. The question of where the boundaries between them should be occupied much of the twentieth century.

For at least the first half of that century, government's role in the economy was expanding in most countries around the world. But the negative consequences led to dramatic movements toward free markets, not only in democratic countries but even in Communist countries, toward the end of that century. Not everyone is convinced of the greater efficiency of the free market, however, even in the twenty-first century. Congressman Dennis Kucinich, for example, declared in 2003:

> Every human being has the right to clean water. . . . I strongly believe that public control and public administration of the public's water supply is the only way to guarantee the universal human right to access to clean water.

Such statements make the difference between political statements and economic analysis stand out in sharp contrast. No doubt both politicians and economists can agree on the desirability of everyone's having water to drink and that it is better when this water is not dirty. But to call water a "right" is meaningless in economic terms and questionable in legal terms. The American Bill of Rights is essentially a list of things that the government is

---

[7]This is discussed in greater detail in my *Knowledge and Decisions*.

prevented from doing to you. Rights in the sense of exemptions from the power of government are very different from rights to things that can be provided only by incurring costs. Your right to free speech does not require someone else to pay for broadcasting what you say or to publish it in a newspaper or magazine. But if you have a right to water, then others are forced to pay the inescapable costs of getting it to you.

This issue then amounts to the question whether water—or food or clothing or anything else—will be better provided to more people if it is paid for collectively through taxes or individually through purchases. Food is as vital to human survival as water is, and yet countries where food has been grown and distributed collectively by government have not been better fed than countries where all this has been left to the marketplace. Indeed, two Soviet economists pointed out that "not until the 1950s were we able to exceed the 1913 per capita level of agricultural output" under the czars, and that even in the late 1980s when they wrote, per capita "meat consumption still remains lower than it was in 1927"— which is to say, before Stalin collectivized agriculture. The Soviet Union was just one of a number of countries that had once had surplus food to export before the government took control of agriculture and which later had food shortages, hunger and sometimes even starvation, and which were forced to import food, even when there was ample fertile soil within the country. People in these countries might have had a right to food, sometimes explicitly specified, but what they were lacking was actual food to go with that right. Conversely, denying people a right to food is not denying them actual food. Countries where food is provided through free markets are often countries where obesity is a far greater problem than malnutrition.

To analyze the market does not preclude the existence of non-market activities or prejudge their effectiveness, any more than automotive engineering precludes the existence or prejudges the effectiveness of alternative modes of transportation. What economic analysis of markets does is utilize a body of knowledge, analysis, and experience that has accumulated and developed over a period of centuries to systematically examine the consequences of various economic actions and policies. The fact that these consequences can determine the poverty or prosperity of millions of people—and billions of people worldwide—is what makes it important to understand economics.

The real question is not which system would work best ideally, but which has in fact produced the better results with far from ideal human beings. Even with the more modest task of evaluating different policies within a given system, the real question is not which policy sounds more plausible, or which would work best if people behaved ideally, but which policy in fact turns out to produce better results with actual people, behaving as they actually do. This latter question will be addressed in different contexts in the chapters that follow.

Chapter 2

Free and Unfree Labor

A student asked his history professor: "Where did slavery come from?"

"You're asking the wrong question," the professor replied. "The real question is: Where did freedom come from?"

Slavery is one of the oldest and most universal of all human institutions. Slavery has existed among peoples around the world, as far back as recorded history goes, and archaeological explorations suggest that it existed before human beings learned to write. *No one knows when slavery began.* It is the idea of freedom for the great masses of ordinary people that is relatively new, as history is measured—and this idea is by no means universally accepted around the world, even today. Slavery was stamped out over most of the world during the course of the nineteenth century, but it still survives here and there in the twenty-first century. Moreover, there have been, and still are, other kinds of unfree labor besides slavery.

One of the many freedoms we take for granted today is the right to choose what kind of work we will and will not do. Yet, for many centuries, there was no such choice for most people in most countries. If you were the son of a shoemaker, then your job would be to make shoes. And if you were the daughter of a farmer, there was a whole range of chores that you would perform while growing up and a still larger range of domestic responsibilities waiting for you after marriage. The difference between "free" and "unfree" labor in such times was whether or not you were paid for your work or were forced to do it without financial compensation. These forced labors might be temporary and range from drudgery in the fields of the nobility or serving under those same nobles in their military campaigns, after which you were allowed to return to your own farming or to other work. People who were less fortunate were full-time and lifelong serfs or slaves, with this status also being inherited by their children.

While free labor has become the norm in much of the world today, compulsory labor still survives, even in free democratic countries, in such forms as military drafts and compulsory jury duty. Outright slavery still exists in a few other countries, such as Mauritania, Sudan, and Nigeria. In remote parts of India, family members still remain in bondage over the generations because of debts contracted by some ancestor before they were born—a situation sometimes called debt peonage and sometimes called simply slavery in one of its variations.

Despite the sharp dichotomy between free and unfree labor in principle, in practice those who are free may nevertheless have many restrictions imposed on them by laws and policies, such as requirements to get an occupational license or belong to a labor union in order to work in some occupations, when in fact both union memberships or the necessary licenses may be arbitrarily limited in numbers. The wholly voluntary agreement between employer and employee in a free market exists as a model but not always as a reality. The employer's freedom to hire whoever will work for him is heavily circumscribed by child labor laws, anti-discrimination laws, and other regulations and policies, as well as by labor union contracts.

At the other end of the spectrum, even some slaves have had options, especially urban slaves, many of whom chose their own employers and simply shared their earnings with slaveowners who let them exercise this option. This practice existed as far back as the Roman Empire, though to varying degrees at different times and places.

FREE LABOR

The advantages of a free labor market benefit not only the worker but also the economy. Since pay is usually based on productivity and workers tend to seek higher-paying jobs, this whole process tends to place people where they can contribute the most to the production of goods and services that other people want. Arbitrary restrictions on who can work where tend to sacrifice not only the interests of those who are denied jobs but also the interests of consumers, who are denied an opportunity to get the goods and services they want in the abundance they would like and at as low a price as possible. Nevertheless, most people would prefer not to see little children working in coal mines, as they once did, or in factories alongside powerful and dangerous machines. Virtually everyone would also prefer not to have anyone who wants to perform surgery be authorized to do so, with or without the benefit of medical training. Some occupations, such as burglar, are banned outright.

In one way or another, for good reasons or bad, there are many restrictions on free labor and on those who employ free labor. Among these restrictions are occupational licensing, job security laws, and minimum wage laws. It should also be noted that much of what is called "labor" is in fact capital.

Human Capital

Most people in modern industrial societies are called workers or labor. However, people represent not only labor but also capital investments. Schooling, job experience, reading, experience gained tinkering with cars or computers, as well as absorbing the knowledge and experience of parents and peers, all contribute to the development of the skills, insights, and capabilities on the job that economists call human capital. Nor is the distinction between human labor and human capital just a set of abstract concepts without consequences.

The ability to labor is usually greatest in early adulthood, when people are in their physical prime. Back in the days when many workers did in fact contribute little more than their physical exertions, a middle-aged manual laborer was typically less employable than a young man in his twenties working in the same occupation. But today, when most people who work for a living earn more as they grow older, this is much more consistent with their earning a return on their human capital, which tends to increase with age. The human capital concept is also more consistent with narrowing income gaps between women and men, as physical strength counts for less and less in an economy where power increasingly comes from machines rather than human muscle, and an economy in which information and high-tech skills count for more.

While the growing importance of human capital tends to create greater equality between the sexes, it tends to create greater inequality between those people who have been assiduous in acquiring knowledge and mastering skills and those who have not. In addition, like every other source of greater rewards for work, it tends to create greater inequality between those who work and those who do not. American families in the bottom 20 percent of income earners supply only a fraction of the hours of work per year supplied by families in the top 20 percent. Both the rising incomes of more experienced workers and the growing inequality in incomes in free market societies show the influence of human capital.

While almost all jobs today provide both pay and experience, at one time it was common for inexperienced and uneducated young people to take jobs that paid them nothing. This was obviously an investment of their time and labor for the sake of acquiring human capital. Apprenticeship, with and without pay, has been a centuries-old institution in many parts of the world, and unpaid labor was not uncommon in the United States as late as the Great Depression of the 1930s, when people desperate for work took jobs without pay for the sake of gaining work experience that would improve their chances of getting paying jobs later.

Back around the time of the First World War, a young black American named Paul Williams decided to become an architect—a virtually unheard of occupation for someone of his race at that time—and turned down the only paying job he was offered at an architectural firm, in order to go to work as an office boy without pay in a more prominent architectural firm, from which he expected to gain more valuable knowledge and experience.[1] He was clearly thinking beyond the initial stage of his career.

As the later stages of his development unfolded, Paul Williams went on to have a long and distinguished career as an architect, in which he designed everything from mansions for movie stars to banks, hotels, and churches, and participated in designing the theme building at the Los Angeles International Airport. Like people who invest money in stocks and bonds, he had invested his time and labor to acquire human capital that paid off as his professional career unfolded.

Another example, from the nineteenth century, was a poverty-stricken young man, dressed in ragged clothes, who applied for a job as sales clerk in a store in upstate New York. His name was

---

[1] After he showed up for work, however, his employer decided to pay him a small salary, after all.

Frank Winfield Woolworth, later destined to become head of a variety store chain that bore his name. But, as of 1873, he was just a very unpromising-looking prospect. Here was the scene:

> The shop owner fingers his mustache thoughtfully. The boy before him is clearly green, but he does seem sincere. Still, times were tough and at least twenty experienced candidates would soon be clamoring for this job.
>
> And all in all, the boy is a sorry excuse for a potential salesman.
>
> But the owner sees something there.
>
> "Okay," he barks. "The job is yours. You start Monday!"
>
> Trying to control his elation, the young man asked: "What are you going to pay me, sir?"
>
> "Pay you!?" the owner exclaims. "You don't expect me to pay you, do you? Why, you should pay me for teaching you the business."

The terms might seem harsh—the first three months with no pay—and even exploitative. But who benefited most from this deal?[2]

Woolworth was a conscientious worker, but he was also a country bumpkin who was so inept that his duties were at first confined to sweeping the floor, dusting the shelves, and doing other work that would not be considered too challenging for him. The other clerks in the store laughed at him. In short, he was being paid about what he was worth. It was a long time before anyone would risk letting him wait on customers.

---

[2]While the employer had the prospect of more experienced job applicants, Woolworth's alternative was to remain on his father's farm. His brother described their routine of going out at 5:30 in the morning to milk the cows, barefoot even on cold mornings: "We would stand on the ground upon which the cows had been lying to get a little warmth into our nearly frozen feet. No wonder we yearned to get away from the endless drudgery."

The three months of working for free—from seven in the morning until nine at night—that Woolworth invested paid off bigger than a lottery. After he became a paid employee, the knowledge and experience which he accumulated working in that store eventually enabled him to go out into the world to set up his own store—and, in the decades ahead, ultimately thousands of stores around the world, which made him one of the most fabulously wealthy men of his time.[3] In later years, he spoke with gratitude of the man who had hired him—and he made his former employer a partner in the F. W. Woolworth retail chain. He indeed ended up paying him for teaching him the business.

In more recent times, minimum wage laws and public disapproval of non-paying jobs have eliminated this particular way of acquiring human capital. However, many people continue to take lower-paying jobs than they could get elsewhere when they value the experience available to them in the less remunerative job and expect to cash in on it later on in their careers. They are thinking beyond stage one.

Some begin administrative careers as modestly paid officials in government regulatory agencies, in order to go on to higher-paying jobs in the industries regulated by those agencies, where their inside knowledge would be valuable to these businesses in coping with numerous government rules and regulations. Some people with Ph.D.s in the sciences may choose to become post-doctoral fellows at prestigious universities, where they can work with world-class chemists or physicists, rather than take a teaching post at a lesser institution where they would receive higher pay than they get from their fellowship. After they have learned from work-

---

[3]The Woolworth Building in New York, once the tallest building in the world, may well still be the only skyscraper in the world whose construction was paid for in cash from the personal fortune of one man, F. W. Woolworth.

ing with top people in their respective fields, their own enhanced reputations can then make them more marketable at higher-level institutions at higher pay.

Those who disdain low-paying jobs as "menial" or who refuse to accept "chump change" for entry-level work are usually not thinking beyond stage one. Not only isolated individuals like Paul Williams or F.W. Woolworth began in this way, so have great numbers of others who have developed human capital and collected the dividends later. A study of Americans in the top one percent of wealth-holders found that the average age at which they began working part-time was fifteen—which suggests that some may well have been working in violation of child labor laws. Despite the assumption of fixed "classes" to which people belong for life, most Americans in lower income brackets do not stay in those brackets for more than a few years.

While upward social mobility has been called "the American Dream," it is by no means confined to Americans—and it is no mere dream. Studies in Greece, Holland, Britain, Canada, and New Zealand have found similar patterns. At the other end of the income scale, when *Forbes* magazine ran its first list of the 400 richest Americans in 1982, that list included 14 Rockefellers, 23 du Ponts and 11 Hunts. Twenty years later, the list included 3 Rockefellers, one Hunt and no du Ponts.

While such patterns are common in Western industrial nations, they are not confined to such nations. Even such a caste-ridden society as India has had some remarkable rags-to riches stories, especially after more free markets emerged toward the end of the twentieth century.[4] While rigid caste lines continue to be observed in rural villages, the cost of doing so in modern, high-tech sectors

---

[4]See, for example, *India Unbound* by Gurcharand Das, Chapters 13 and 17.

of the Indian economy would include passing up huge profits that could be made by employing the talents of scientists, engineers, inventors, and entrepreneurs who might not have originated in the highest social levels.

Ironically, the notion of fixed "classes" to which people belong has acquired widespread influence at a time when increasing evidence from around the world belies that assumption. While it has become fashionable in many quarters to sneer at the idea of economic opportunity and upward mobility—fashion and sneers being substitutes for knowledge—the evidence keeps piling up that income mobility is the rule, not the exception, in free market economies. As Professor Peter Bauer of the London School of Economics remarked, "British industry is managed, and has been managed for decades or even centuries by new men, people who have made their own way, often from humble beginnings." But apparently such facts have not greatly changed popular perceptions. Professor Bauer also noted: "Indeed, it is quite usual to read accounts in the newspapers of the careers of very rich people who have started with nothing, side by side with articles complaining of the rigid class structure in Britain."

Young people who begin by working at McDonald's seldom spend their careers at McDonald's. Just in the course of a year, McDonald's has more than a 100 percent turnover rate. What those who leave take with them is not only such basic experience as showing up for work regularly, cooperating with others, and knowing how to conduct themselves in a business environment, but also a track record that enables them to move on to other and very different occupations at progressively higher levels in the years ahead. The experience and the track record from McDonald's are likely to be more valuable in the long run than the modest paychecks they earned serving hamburgers.

Put differently, whatever reduces opportunities for gainful employment for people with little or no experience has the effect of costing both them and the society far more than the lost jobs which have been dismissed as "menial" or as paying only "chump change." Nothing is easier than to take a lofty moral position that when minimum wage laws, for example, result in a reduction of low-paying jobs, it is nothing to regret, as some politicians and journalist have done:

> People who get up and go to work each day deserve to make enough money to cover their essential needs. Employers that aren't productive enough to provide such a basic level of compensation—"chiselers," some detractors have called them—don't belong in an affluent society.

Having wage rates set by third parties' notions of workers' "essential needs" would be a radical departure from having wages set by supply and demand—and it is by no means clear how either the allocation of resources in the economy or the interests of the workers themselves would be better served in this way. These workers may well feel that their most "essential need" is a job and that destroying both jobs and the employers who provide them solves none of the workers' problems. The only clear beneficiaries would be those who acquire such arbitrary powers over their fellow human beings and are thus able to feel both important and noble while in fact leaving havoc in their wake.

Obviously, those people who are working for employers whom third party observers regard as expendable would not be working for them if there were better alternatives available. How does removing one of the options of people with few options make them better off? Similar one-stage thinking is also apparent in many observers who wax indignant over low-wage workers employed in the Third World by multinational corporations. While the pay of such workers is often low by comparison with that of workers in more affluent industrial societies, so too is their productivity. An international consulting firm determined that the average labor productivity in the modern sectors in India is 15 percent of that in the United States.

In other words, if you hired an average Indian worker and paid him one-fifth of what you paid an average American worker, it would cost you *more* to get a given amount of work done in India than in the United States. Paying 20 percent of what an American worker earns to someone who produces only 15 percent of what an American worker produces increases your labor costs, even though you are hiring "cheap labor" and are virtually certain to be accused of "exploitation."

There are reasons why output per worker is much lower in some countries than in others, and the reasons need not be a lack of effort or intelligence on the part of the workers. The amount and quality of the equipment used by the worker, the level of sophistication in the management of the enterprise, and even the higher shipping costs in countries with poor roads and other inadequate infrastructure, all play a role. Management has much to do with the productivity of labor. Companies in Britain run by American managements have had more than 50 percent higher productivity than British companies run by British management.

In Third World countries with poor roads and inefficient rail lines, the net value of the goods shipped is reduced by the additional shipping costs that these entail. Poorer countries often also have higher levels of corruption, including a need to pay numerous bribes in order to do business without being delayed or harassed by officials enforcing innumerable regulations and red tape requirements. Since the value of the worker who produces widgets is based on how much money a widget adds to his employer's revenue, the worker will be worth less when transportation and other costs are higher.

The widget itself may sell for the same price in the world market, whether produced in the Third World or in a modern industrial nation, but the costs of getting the widget from the factory to the point of sale must be deducted in both cases. When that deduction is larger in a country with less efficient transportation and more corrupt officials, the net value of the widget to the enterprise producing it is less—and therefore so is the value of the labor that made it.

Multinational corporations already pay about double the local wage levels in Third World countries, even though they do not pay as much as workers receive in more industrialized nations. Insisting that multinational corporations raise their employees' pay scales in these Third World countries may sound good to those who do not think beyond stage one. But the consequences of such higher pay scales being imposed by law or public pressure can be that it becomes economically preferable for the multinational corporation to discontinue hiring many Third World workers whose output is worth less than what third parties want them paid. This in turn means that Third World workers lose not only jobs that pay more than their local alternatives but also that they lose the human capital that they could acquire from working in more efficient enterprises.

Contrary to theories of "exploitation," most multinational corporations focus the bulk of their operations in countries where pay scales are high, rather than in countries where pay scales are low. The United States, for example, invests far more in the affluent, high-wage countries of Europe and Japan than in India or in all of poverty-stricken sub-Saharan Africa. While those who fear exploitation of low-wage workers may regard that as a good thing, it is in fact tragic that so many desperately poor people are denied both much-needed income and opportunities to increase their human capital and, with it, their countries' prospects for future prosperity. To the extent that their would-be benefactors succeed in raising their pay scales without being able to raise their productivity, the net result is likely to be pricing them out of jobs. As a noted economist once said: "We cannot make a man worth a given amount by making it illegal for anyone to offer him less."

Job Security

Another area in which failing to think beyond stage one promotes policies whose unintended consequences backfire is that of job security laws and policies imposed by governments or labor unions. The obvious purpose of such laws is to reduce unemployment but that is very different from saying that this is their actual effect.

Job security laws and policies restrict an employer's ability to lay off workers for economic reasons or to fire them for unsatisfactory work. In India, for example, engineers in the government-owned telephone system have been guaranteed lifetime jobs, even if the phone system is someday privatized. It is much the same story in Poland, where the sale of state-owned enterprises from the Communist era to foreign investors has had preconditions such as a four-year "no layoff" agreement for France Telecom when it bought a Polish telecommunications firm, and a ten-year moratorium on layoffs for workers in a Polish power plant bought by a Belgian company. Germany's job-protection laws and mandatory benefits to workers have made labor costs in German industry "the world's highest," according to *The Economist* magazine and "arguably the biggest single obstacle to job-creation."

Although such laws protect workers who already have jobs, nevertheless the increased labor costs created by these laws discourage the investments needed to create jobs for workers who do not yet have jobs. These laws make it more profitable to buy labor-saving

machines and to work existing workers overtime when more output is needed, rather than hire additional workers whom it would
be difficult to lay off when output returned to previous levels.
Countries with such job security laws typically do not have lower
unemployment rates but instead higher unemployment rates than
countries without such job protection. It is a classic example of
stage one benefits, followed by losses at later stages.

An extreme example of what government may be willing to do
with the taxpayers' money was a state-owned fertilizer plant in India, which continued to employ thousands of workers for years,
even though the plant produced no fertilizer whatever:

> The cleaning crew kept the factory clean, the mechanics kept the
> machinery in good order, and the workshop supplied spare parts.
> The managers and workers came to work, and the personnel depart-
> ment marked attendance. Everyone was paid, including a bonus,
> and even overtime in some cases. However, they had no work be-
> cause soon after the factory was built it was discovered that the
> company was unviable. If they had produced, they would have lost
> masses of money. It was cheaper not to produce. Yet they could not
> close down. Not only was it bad politics to close, the law did not
> permit it.

Given such laws and practices, it is not surprising that, while
more than half of India's industrial work force worked for government-owned enterprises in 1990, they produced only 27 percent of
the country's industrial output that year. Job security laws often
mean low productivity and low productivity means lower standards
of living for the country as a whole.

The particular job security policies in American colleges and
universities have their own peculiar consequences, often quite different from the goals of these policies. Academics who have been

employed a given number of years at a given college or university must either be promoted to a position with permanent tenure or let go. This is called the "up or out" system. It means more job security for those who go up but less job security for those who are forced out—less not only compared to their more fortunate academic colleagues, but less compared to people of similar ages in other sectors of the economy without such job security systems.

Because academic job security systems leave colleges and universities with long-term commitments that can easily exceed a million dollars for each tenured faculty member, this can lead to more stringent requirements for continued employment than if no such commitment were implied. In other words, untenured faculty members whose current work is perfectly satisfactory will often be let go—not have their contracts renewed—when time comes for the "up or out" decision, when there is not yet sufficient evidence to be confident that this person will in future years progress to the higher performance levels expected of senior faculty members, notably in scholarly research.

In the absence of this "up or out" system, people who are perfectly satisfactory as assistant professors could continue to be employed as assistant professors, while others could progress onward and upward to become associate professors or full professors at whatever time their work merited such promotions, whether that was before or after the number of years established for making "up or out" decisions under the current system. Those who never reached the higher levels of performance required for such promotions could nevertheless continue to be employed at their current level, so long as their work was satisfactory at that level.

In other words, people who would be able to keep their jobs in the absence of the current academic job security system instead lose their jobs because this job security system imposes long-term commitments that colleges and universities seek to avoid by retaining only those young faculty members whose promise seems great enough and clear enough, soon enough.

At the highest-rated universities, it is common for *most* assistant professors to be terminated before time for them to become associate professors, since there has seldom been enough time for them to have produced the high levels of research quantity and quality required for senior positions at such institutions. In short, the difference between the goal of a policy—in this case, greater job security—turns out to have little to do with the actual outcome of that policy, which is less job security than most people of similar ages have in other sectors of the economy where there are no such policies.

This academic promotions system also helps explain a common but paradoxical phenomenon at many universities—the outstanding young teacher who is terminated, to the consternation of his students, who may even mount organized protests, usually in vain. It is even common on some campuses to hear the "teacher of the year" award referred to as "the kiss of death" for young faculty members. That is because outstanding teaching is very time-consuming, in terms of creating high-quality courses and preparing each lecture in these courses, so that there is insufficient time left for doing the amount and quality of research required for getting tenure at a top university. Such institutions usually fill their senior positions by hiring those people who have already produced the requisite quantity and quality of publications somewhere else.

Crime as an Occupation

Perhaps the freest of all occupations is that of the career criminal, who simply ignores the restrictions that the law attempts to impose. While many crimes are committed by people in a moment of passion or a moment when temptations overcome both morality and logic, the person whose whole livelihood depends on the com-

While 13 percent of burglaries in the United States occur while the home is occupied, more than 40 percent of the burglaries in Britain, the Netherlands, and Canada occur while the home is occupied. These latter three countries have much lower incidences of gun ownership than the United States, due to more severe gun control laws. After the Atlanta suburb of Kennesaw passed an ordinance requiring heads of households to keep a firearm in their homes, residential burglaries dropped by 89 percent.

Another major cost to a criminal career is the danger of incurring legal penalties, usually imprisonment. Here criminal activity in general has tended to vary inversely with the risk of imprisonment. In the United States, various legal reforms of the 1960s had the net effect of reducing the likelihood that anyone committing a given crime would actually spend time behind bars as a result. Crime rates skyrocketed. The murder rate, for example, was twice as high in 1974 as in 1961, and between 1960 and 1976 a citizen's chance of becoming a victim of some major violent crime tripled.

Data from other countries show similar trends. On a graph showing the rate of crime in Australia from 1964 to 1999 and the rate of imprisonment per 1,000 crimes committed over that same span, the two lines are virtually mirror-images of one another, with the rate of imprisonment going down and the rate of crime going up. The graphs for England and Wales, New Zealand, and the United States are very similar. In the United States, the crime rate peaked in the 1980s and began falling as the rate of incarceration rose. In England and Wales, the rate of imprisonment hit bottom in the early 1990s—which is when the crime rate peaked and then began a substantial decline as the rate of imprisonment rose. In New Zealand, the high point in crime was reached in the early 1990s while the low point in incarceration was reached about 1985 mission of crimes is a very different phenomenon. The career criminal cannot simply be dismissed as irrational because there is too much evidence from too many countries that he is indeed quite rational.

It is easy enough to say that "crime does not pay," but the real question is: Does not pay whom—and compared to what? It is doubtful whether Bill Gates could have done nearly as well as he has by becoming a burglar or even a hit man for organized crime, but those who do pursue these criminal occupations are unlikely to have had the same alternatives that Bill Gates had because of his particular talents and circumstances. Given the low educational levels of many who become career criminals, crime may well be their best-paying option. Given the short time horizons of many of those who make crime their occupation—especially young people and people from lower social classes—such things as selling drugs may be very lucrative in stage one, whether or not it leads to prison in stage two or perhaps never living to see stage two.

The rationality of the career criminal is demonstrated in many ways, including a variation in the amount and kinds of crime committed as the costs of committing those crimes vary. These costs include not only the legal penalties but also the dangers faced from potential victims of these crimes. For example, burglary tends to be affected by the proportion of people who have guns in their homes. The rate of burglary is not only much higher in Britain than in the United States—nearly twice as high—British burglars are far less likely than American burglars to "case" the premises before entering, in order to make sure that no one is home. Even if someone is home in Britain, there is far less danger that the person at home will have a firearm, given the far more strict British gun control laws. British and American burglars are both behaving rationally, given the respective circumstances in which they operate.

and then began to rise again, with the crime rate falling with a lag of a few years.

This is not to say that crime is unaffected by cultural or other differences among these countries, even though historically they are all offshoots of the same British culture. There are serious cultural differences which are no doubt reflected in the *absolute* levels of crime, though the similarity in *trends* is very striking.

As one example of absolute levels of crime that cannot be explained by laws, in the nineteenth century, guns were freely available in both London and New York City, and yet the murder rate in New York was several times what it was in London. Early in the twentieth century, severe gun control laws were passed in New York State before such laws were imposed in England—and yet New York City continued to have several times as high a murder rate as London.

Eventually, Britain's gun control laws were tightened far more so than those in the United States, especially after the Second World War. Yet Britain's crime rates in general, and murder rates in particular, rose as these gun control laws became ever tighter in the latter part of the twentieth century. However, because New York's murder rate continued to be far higher than that in London, and that in the United States far higher than that in Britain, this differential was often attributed to differences in gun control laws. In reality, the United States has lower murder rates than some other countries with stronger gun control laws, such as Russia, as well as higher murder rates than other countries with stronger gun control laws, such as Britain.

While there are undoubtedly many complex factors behind the absolute crime rates in any country, the trends strongly suggest that changes in crime rates reflect rational reactions to those changes by criminals.

UNFREE LABOR

Involuntary labor can range from jury duty to military draftees to inmates of forced labor camps to outright chattel slavery, in which people are bought and sold like cattle.

The power of American courts to force citizens to serve on juries has even been used to send out law enforcement officers to seize customers at random in shopping centers, taking them directly to court to fill in as jurors, when there have been inadequate numbers of jurors on hand to conduct trials. While this is an extreme example, it demonstrates the government's power to compel involuntary labor. According to a news item in the *Wall Street Journal*:

> Michael Kanz was pushing a grocery cart toward the checkout lane at the Wal-Mart Supercenter here when a woman wearing a gun walked up and told him to follow her orders—or face the consequences.
>
> It wasn't a mugging, but a jury summons to report to court within an hour. And it's a perfectly legal way some judges have in recent years been getting jurors at the last minute.

The various categories of involuntary labor differ not only in duration but also in severity. Jurors do not usually serve as long as military draftees, and inmates of forced labor camps may serve for years but not necessarily for a lifetime, as slaves usually did. The severity of treatment also varies, being more severe for draftees than for jurors, and often more severe for inmates of government-run forced labor camps than for privately owned slaves, whose long-term productivity would be jeopardized by very severe treatment. But, because people in forced labor camps are not owned by anyone, their long-term productivity matters less—if at all—to the decision-makers directly in charge of them, who have no incentive to think beyond stage one.

Productivity of Involuntary Labor

In some forced labor camps, especially those run by the Nazis and the Japanese during World War II, the inmates were often simply worked literally to death. The same was true of most Chinese indentured servants sent to Cuba in the nineteenth century. In both cases, as well as in the Soviet gulags of the twentieth century, total control and an absence of ownership meant that the long-run productivity of these workers meant nothing to those in charge of them, who had no incentive to think beyond stage one. Only where privately owned slaves were very cheap and easily replaced were they likely to be worked at a literally killing pace or subjected to dangerous working conditions. Where they were expensive and not easily replaced, as in the American antebellum South, the need to preserve the existing slaves often led their owners to hire Irish immigrants to do work considered too dangerous for slaves.

During Frederick Law Olmsted's celebrated travels through the antebellum South, he was puzzled to see black slaves throwing 500-pound bales of cotton down an incline to Irish workers who were at the bottom, catching these bales and loading them onto a boat. When Olmsted asked about this racial division of labor, he was told that slaves "are worth too much to be risked here; if the Paddies are knocked over board, or get their backs broke, nobody loses anything." It was likewise common to use the Irish for other work considered too dangerous for slaves, such as draining swamps that might be malarial, building levees that might collapse on the workmen, building railroads, or tending steam boilers that might blow up.

How does involuntary labor in general affect the allocation of scarce resources which have alternative uses—and therefore the economic wellbeing of the country as a whole? Because involuntary labor, by definition, does not have to be paid a price reflecting the value of the alternative uses of its time and capabilities, such labor is often used for work that is less valuable than its alternative uses. A chemist may be drafted into the army and then used as a clerk handling clothing supplies in the quartermaster corps. In an all-volunteer army, it would be cheaper for the military authorities to hire a civilian to perform such clerical duties than to pay enough to attract chemists or other highly skilled people to do this routine work.

If military personnel were used for such work in a volunteer army, these would more likely be individuals whose civilian skill levels were low enough that the army could attract them at considerably lower pay than would be required to attract people like chemists. Such financial considerations taken into account by military authorities would reflect more fundamental underlying realities from the standpoint of the economy as a whole: Involuntary labor is a less efficient way to allocate scarce resources which have alternative uses.

People summoned to jury duty may have great amounts of their time wasted waiting around to be told whether they will in fact be seated as jurors for pending cases on a given day or ordered to keep coming back on subsequent days until their tour of jury duty has been served. Moreover, what they are paid is usually far below what they earn in their regular occupations. More fundamentally, they may sit on cases whose importance to the larger society may be less than the value of what they would be contributing otherwise in their regular lines of work. Such considerations tend to lead people in higher paid professions to seek to avoid jury duty by utilizing whatever exemptions or excuses may be available, while retirees or people in lower-level occupations may find jury duty less of a burden, and perhaps more interesting than alternative uses of their time.

As with the service of military draftees, the cost of involuntary labor to decision-making authorities understates its cost to the economy as a whole, and thereby results in misallocation of scarce resources. In the case of juries, the lesser likelihood of people from higher occupations ending up serving as jurors can also reduce the quality of jury decisions, to the detriment of justice.

Forced Labor Camps

One of the largest and longest lasting systems of involuntary labor in the twentieth century was that of the forced labor camps—the gulags—in the Soviet Union. As of 1949, for example, there were well over 2 million prisoners in Soviet forced labor camps. Because of turnover, due both to releases and incarceration of new prisoners, as well as substantial numbers of deaths within the gulags, the total number of forced laborers over a period of decades was many times that.

Both inhumanity and inefficiency were hallmarks of these camps. Deaths averaged more than 50,000 prisoners per month in the particularly bad year of 1942, from a combination of overwork, malnutrition, mistreatment, and harsh climatic conditions with inadequate clothing. During the war years as a whole, more than 2 million people died in Soviet prison camps—more than the number of Soviet citizens and soldiers who died as prisoners of the invading Nazis and their allies.

Despite the long hours of work and inadequate food, clothing, housing, and medical care that contributed to staggering death rates, the forced labor of the inmates still did not cover the costs of the gulags. Shortly after Stalin's death, the head of the Soviet secret police—hardly a humanitarian—began closing the camps down for economic reasons. Those who ran the gulags had unbridled power over the inmates but did not own them or their output as property, so they had no incentives to be efficient. As a Soviet official described it:

As a rule, the plans are unrealistic, the requests for workers exceed that required for the plan severalfold, but the Gulag grants these requests, that is, in other words, the branch administration do not value their workforce; they believe that, since the Gulag is right there with a ready reserve of workers, they can be wasteful with the workforce, to use it at any time and in any way they wish.

Because of the sheer size and scope of the gulag system, it made huge contributions to various parts of the Soviet economy, but usually at far higher costs than those of comparable enterprises in the general economy. In its heyday, forced labor in the Soviet Union produced one-fourth of all the country's timber, 40 percent of its cobalt, 60 percent of its gold and 76 percent of its tin. Forced labor also produced coal, oil, and gas, and built many canals and even apartment buildings in Moscow, among many other economic activities. But just the purely economic costs—quite aside from the staggering human costs—were typically higher than the cost of doing the same things outside the gulags. For example, the cost of producing bricks in a facility with forced labor was more than double the cost of producing them in a nearby Soviet brick factory. In addition, the gulags were "notoriously reckless in their use of natural resources," according to a scholar at the Russian Academy of Sciences in Moscow. All of this was consistent with the incentives and constraints facing them, however much it violated both economic and humanitarian principles.

With the opening of the government's secret archives in the last years of the Soviet Union, the extent of the inefficiencies of forced labor were more fully revealed. The building of railroads was an example:

By 1938 the length of railroads on which construction had been started but had been suspended was approaching 5,000 km (not counting railroads that had been completed but were unused or partially used because they were unneeded). Meanwhile, the total increase in the USSR's railroad system between 1933 and 1939 amounted to a mere 4,500 km. A considerable portion of the "dead railroads" was built at the cost of many prisoners' lives.

Slavery

Slavery has existed on every inhabited continent and among people of every race for thousands of years. The very word "slave" derives from the word for Slav, not only in the English language but also in other European languages and in Arabic. That is because so many Slavs were enslaved for centuries before the first African was brought to the Western Hemisphere in bondage.

The roles played by slaves have covered an enormous spectrum. Some were used as human sacrifices by the Aztecs of Central America or in Indonesia or in parts of Africa, among other places. In the Roman Empire, some slaves were forced to fight each other to the death as gladiators, for the entertainment of crowds in the Coliseum. After Europeans took over the Western Hemisphere, most African slaves brought there were used for routine manual labor, such as growing sugar cane in tropical countries or cotton in the American antebellum South. Yet, in various parts of the world and in various periods of history, slave roles have ranged all the way up to that of imperial viceroys and commanders of armies in the Ottoman Empire.

As a general pattern, the more highly skilled, the more intellectually demanding, and the more responsible the roles filled by slaves, the less they were treated with the brutality and contempt inflicted on slaves doing arduous manual labor. In short, although freedom and slavery are a stark contrast in principle, in practice there were degrees of slavery. In countries around the world, slaves who were domestic servants tended to be treated better than those who were field hands or other manual laborers, and those in higher level occupations tended to be less and less treated as slaves, while for some at the highest levels their bondage was nominal.

Slaves used as divers in the Carolina swamps, for example, had to exercise skill and discretion and were accordingly treated differently from plantation slaves, being rewarded with both financial incentives and with greater personal freedom on and off the job. Similarly with slaves in lumbering operations or the processing of tobacco, which likewise required skill and discretion. In one remarkable case, a slave was made captain of a river boat, with a crew of both black and white sailors under his command. These more responsible jobs often also offered more opportunities for escape, which in turn meant that severe treatment of such slaves would have been counterproductive and was therefore much less common than on plantations where slaves performed routine manual labor.

Urban slaves in general were also treated less harshly for the same reason and Frederick Douglass described the typical urban slave in the antebellum South as "almost a free citizen." But being *almost* free was not the same as being free. Some, like Douglass himself, decided to become fully free citizens by escaping. While permanent escape from a slave plantation was very rare—perhaps two percent of the slaves made good their escapes without being recaptured—escapes by urban slaves were far more often permanently successful. Slaveowners who thought beyond stage one had to take into account the increased possibilities of escape, as well as other costs such as financial incentives and better working conditions for slaves doing higher level work. Obviously, the increased value of that work had to be great enough to cover these additional costs and risks.

These modifications of slavery implicitly recognized the inefficiencies of pure unmitigated slavery. For routine work that was easily monitored, such as growing sugar cane or cotton, slavery could extract the necessary efforts under the threat of the lash. But for anything requiring judgment, initiative, and talent, other incentives must be invoked, simply because it is hard for someone else to know how much potential for judgment, initiative, or talent any other given individual has. Economic and other rewards cause the individual to reveal those qualities in exchange for being treated less like a slave and rewarded in other ways.

Where slave populations were large enough to have a serious potential for social disruption and danger to the lives of the free population, the need to minimize such dangers limited the extent to which the slave population could be educated for higher roles, since such education could also facilitate organized disruptions, escapes, and uprisings among the enslaved people. Therefore educating slaves was forbidden by law throughout the Western Hemisphere in post-Columbian times. From an economic standpoint, this meant that, in addition to inefficiencies in using people of a given capability, slavery also limited the capabilities that could be developed among people of a given potential. Put differently, freedom has not only personal and political benefits, but economic benefits as well.

Markets for Involuntary Labor

The wasteful use of unowned involuntary labor can be contrasted with the more careful allocation of involuntary labor that is owned and sold, since both buyer and seller in free market economies have financial incentives to weigh the productivity of the labor in alternative uses. However, the desire of those held involuntarily to be free imposes costs to keeping them in bondage, and these costs must be deducted from whatever gains their owners receive from their involuntary labor.

Slaves are not the only involuntary labor that is bought and sold. The services of German mercenaries, such as those who were used by the British in their attempt to suppress the American revolution, were sold or rented collectively by heads of the various German principalities of the time, who treated these soldiers as if they were property. Serfs were bought and sold as part of the land traded among medieval European landowners. Prison labor has been used by both public organizations and private individuals in the United States, well into the twentieth century.

Much of the white population of seventeenth-century colonial America—more than half in colonies south of New England—arrived as indentured servants, sometimes having contracted individually to work a specified number of years for those who had paid their passage across the Atlantic, and more often having indentured themselves to the owners of the ships that brought them to America, so that the captains of these ships then auctioned them off after reaching land, much as slaves were auctioned. Another variation on these arrangements was that the passengers would pay as much of the fare as they could and would then depend on family or friends to pay the rest when they arrived in America—failing which, they would then be auctioned off with other indentured servants.

Indentured labor was common in the Caribbean as well as in the American colonies and continued to be an important source of labor from India and China to various parts of the world, well into the nineteenth century. By 1859, only the Portuguese port of Macao on the south China coast continued to ship indentured servants from that country—but they shipped large numbers. In the quarter century beginning in 1849, approximately 90,000 Chinese indentured laborers were shipped from Macao to Peru alone. Another 125,000 were shipped to Cuba during the period from 1847 to 1874. Most of the Chinese shipped to these countries never saw China again and the brutal conditions of their labor in Cuba were such that most died before completing the eight years of their labor contracts. Things were not much better in Peru, where guards were posted to prevent suicide among the Chinese shovelling bird manure into sacks for export as fertilizer, under conditions of stifling heat and stench. Suicides were common, beginning in the holding pens back in Macao, where some of these prisoners were seen "dripping with blood" as a result of punishments meted out to them. The suicides continued during the months-long voyages across the Pacific. Many of these Chinese had been tricked, drugged, or otherwise forced into these indentures—as had also been true of many seventeenth-century Britons, including children, who were brought to the Western Hemisphere involuntarily.

Indentured laborers and other forms of contract labor were usually a result of initially free choices, however, even if their subsequent assignments to individual purchasers or to particular tasks were no longer a matter of individual free choice on their part. The Portuguese trade in indentured—often coerced—labor from China was, fortunately, exceptional. Many, if not most, of the millions of emigrants from India to various parts of the world in the nineteenth century left as indentured laborers under contract. The fact that they not only completed these contracts but often renewed their contracts, either immediately or after returning to India for a sojourn, suggests that their treatment, though usually far from ideal, was not under such desperate conditions as to lead to suicides on a large scale.

Most of the elements of choice open to most indentured workers were lacking in the markets for slaves, where the choices were entirely in the hands of the buyers and sellers. This did not mean that the choices made by slave traders and slave owners were unconstrained expressions of personal whims, because they were constrained by economic considerations in general and by supply and demand in particular.

Costs of Enslavement

Costs are crucially involved in the very choice of whom to enslave in the first place. It is obviously more costly to try to enslave people who have the army and navy of a major nation around them—costly not only in terms of the money and lives expended trying to capture such people, but costly also in the risk of provoking retaliatory military action against the country that launched the slave raids. Broadly speaking, such costs defined those whom it was economically feasible to enslave and those whose costs of capture were prohibitively expensive. From the demand side, there must also be a sufficiently valued use for slaves to cover the costs of even moderately costly enslavement.

In some times and places, slaves were a by-product of military actions undertaken for other purpose. In ancient times, especially, captured enemy soldiers could be killed, sold back to their country for ransom, sold in slave markets, or kept as slaves for use by those who captured them. Here it is not feasible to calculate the separate cost of capturing such slaves, since the costs of military operations were paid for other reasons and had other objectives and consequences. However, campaigns specifically undertaken to capture and enslave other people were more clearly constrained by costs. Moreover, these costs did not remain constant over time. Where small, scattered, tribal societies evolved into larger and more powerful states, the peoples within such societies became less and less likely to be targets of enslavement, as the costs of slave raids rose.

Since some societies evolved in this way and others did not, or evolved more slowly for one reason or another, those peoples likely to be enslaved changed over the centuries. In ancient times, when Britain was a primitive island, fragmented into tribal regions, Julius Caesar raided Britain and brought British slaves back to Rome but, in later centuries, after Britain had a government, an army and a navy, it would be too costly a place to raid for the sake of capturing slaves. However, many parts of the world were more difficult to consolidate into large states, sometimes because of geographic factors creating isolation in mountainous regions or on small islands spread across a vast sea. These more vulnerable regions remained major sources of slaves, whether in Europe, Asia, Africa, the Polynesian islands or the Western Hemisphere.

One such area was the Balkans, whose Slavic inhabitants were enslaved on a large scale for at least six centuries before the first African was brought to the Western Hemisphere in bondage. People were enslaved where the cost of enslaving them was less. For centuries that usually meant that Europeans enslaved other Europeans, Asians enslaved other Asians, Africans enslaved other Africans, and the indigenous peoples of the Western Hemisphere enslaved other indigenous peoples of the Western Hemisphere. Only in relatively recent centuries, as local sources of supply of slaves dried up with the consolidation of nation-states, and as growing wealth enabled people to be enslaved at greater distances and transported far away, did Africa become the principal source of supply for Europeans who transported them across the Atlantic.

Slave Prices

Even slaves destined for lowly manual labor were not simply labor but also represented human capital. Thus a slave in the American antebellum South cost about thirty times what he cost on the coast of Africa, and not all of that was due to transportation costs or even to an allowance for those who died en route. At a minimum, a slave in the United States had to be able to understand the English language. He also had to understand a new work routine, new work implements, and a living pattern different from those in Africa. The whole process of making these adjustments and acquiring various forms of human capital was known as "seasoning" and it often took place in the Caribbean before slaves were sold on the American mainland. Subsequent generations of slave descendants, raised in the new setting, would likewise command higher prices than someone new from Africa for the same reasons.

In addition to this more or less general human capital, some slaves possessed such specific skills as carpentry or animal husbandry, and these commanded a still higher price. In the Ottoman Empire, eunuchs were in great demand to work in the harems of the wealthy and, because most of the slaves who were castrated died, the price of the survivors had to cover all the costs incurred capturing and transporting those who did not survive, so eunuchs were the highest priced slaves of all. Slave prices also varied with the distance from the source, so that slaves in the United States— the most distant of the Western Hemisphere societies holding slaves from Africa—had higher prices than those in Brazil, which was closest to Africa.

One consequence of this difference in prices was that the slave population in Brazil never reproduced itself, but was replenished with new arrivals from Africa, while the slave population in the American South began reproducing themselves and increasing in size as early as colonial times. That is because Brazilian slaveowners found it cheaper to get new slaves from Africa than to raise a new generation from the existing slave population. Thus, in Brazil, there was not only an overwhelmingly male slave population, but also a separation of the sexes, and such slave women as became pregnant were not given as much time off, or sufficiently lighter work, to enable them to ensure the survival of their offspring. In the American South, where the costs of slaves was higher, it paid the slaveowners to have slaves live in families and to lighten the chores of pregnant women to the extent necessary for them to bear and raise the next generation, who represented capital assets to the slaveowners. The American South therefore became one of the few slave societies in the Western Hemisphere where the slave population reproduced itself at a level sufficient to replace existing generations.

The magnitude of the difference made by these different prices, and the different treatment resulting from them, may be indicated by the fact that Brazil imported six times as many slaves from Africa as the United States did, but the resident slave population in the United States was larger than that in Brazil. Even a small group of islands like the West Indies imported more slaves than the United States, despite the fact that the resident slave population in the United States was the largest in the hemisphere. Another example of the effect of economic incentives was in the treatment of slaves on plantations where the slaveowner was in residence, as distinguished from their treatment on plantations run by an overseer serving an absentee owner.

Incentives and Constraints

Overseers tended to be paid by immediate results, such as the output of sugar in the tropics or cotton in the American South. Therefore the overseer had little incentive to think beyond stage one. Special care for pregnant women or the spending of plantation resources on the raising of children who were not yet old enough to produce enough output to cover their upkeep was therefore not something that overseers serving absentee owners had an incentive to do. Even for able-bodied men, the overseer serving an absentee owner had incentives to work them at a pace that would maximize output during his tenure, even if this wore them out at an early age and left them less productive in later life. It was the same story when it came to maintenance and repairs on the plantation or the care of animals or the soil.

In all these ways, plantations with resident owners tended to operate more efficiently in long-run terms—with the people, the animals, the soil, and the structures and equipment better maintained, even if that meant somewhat less output than if everything was sacrificed for immediate production. While most plantations in the American South had resident owners, who could see to it that overseers did not sacrifice the owners' long-run interests to the overseers' immediate interest in getting paid for maximum output and getting a reputation for "results" that would serve as the overseers' capital asset in finding his next job. In the West Indies, however, it was more common for the plantation owners to live in Britain, leaving resident overseers a far freer hand in making decisions. One consequence was that the infant mortality rate among slave women in the West Indies was some multiple of what it was among slave women in the American South.

Slaves and Wealth

In many parts of the world, slaves were bought for their ability to produce wealth that could be appropriated by the slaveowners. Elsewhere, especially in parts of the Middle East, slaveowners often had large numbers of slaves as a sign of the wealth they already possessed. These slaves served as servants, concubines, entertainers, or providers of other amenities—in short, as consumers rather than producers, of wealth. In other kinds of societies, such as those of the Western Hemisphere, where slaves were primarily used as producers of wealth, just how much wealth was actually produced by slavery as an economic system has been a matter of controversy among scholars.

That the slaveowners gained wealth seems clear but whether the whole society gained is less clear. In Brazil and the United States, which had the two largest slave populations in the hemisphere, the regions of these countries where slavery was concentrated—northern Brazil and the southern United States—remained noticeably poorer during the era of slavery and for generations thereafter. The side effects of slavery were not negligible, especially in the United States, where the staggering economic and human costs of the Civil War seemed to fit Abraham Lincoln's premonition that all the treasure built up from unpaid labor might be sunk in the ensuing war and every drop of blood drawn by the lash might be repaid in blood shed with the sword.

The Economics of Freedom

A given individual's value as a free worker was likely to be greater than that same person's value as a slave, because of the constraints inherent in keeping someone in bondage. Whole categories of work were usually off-limits to Western Hemisphere slaves, such as work requiring extensive travel alone, or work requiring the use of firearms, or the handling of large sums of money—all of which could facilitate escape. Education was also both an instrument and an incitement to freedom. Hence its ban for slaves throughout the Western Hemisphere. This, however, then limited still further the kind and quality of work that could be performed by slaves, even when the individuals were perfectly capable of performing these same functions as free workers.

It is a common principle in economics that assets tend to move through the market to their highest valued uses, since that is where the bidding for them will be highest. Accordingly, the economic value of a slave would be greatest to the slave himself, even aside from the value of freedom, as such, while others could own the economic value of a slave, only that individual could own his higher economic value as a free worker. Therefore an ideal free market would lead to slaves buying their own freedom, since they would have an incentive to outbid others on economic grounds alone, even aside from their desire for freedom. Some slaves have in fact done this in many places and times, whether in ancient Rome or centuries later in the Western Hemisphere. Even where slaves have had no money or inadequate amounts of money, ways have been found to arrange self-purchase on credit, to be repaid on the installment plan after achieving freedom. In those societies which gave legal recognition to property owned by slaves—the *peculium*, as it was called in ancient Rome—slaves might in some circumstances earn and save enough over the years to purchase their own freedom for cash.

The practical institutional difficulties of achieving self-purchase were not the only reasons why this procedure was not more widely used, which could have eroded the whole system of slavery. Where the political authorities did not want a large population of ex-slaves of a different race living among the free population, legal restrictions impeded manumission by purchase or grant. Such restrictions became increasingly severe in the American antebellum South during the decades leading up to the Civil War. Thus blacks who had acquired freedom, by purchase or otherwise, often owned other members of their own family as a legal formality, simply because the costs and difficulties of getting them official free-dom papers were so great. Some Southern whites who did not be-lieve in slavery, such as the Quakers, likewise often owned slaves as a formality, while it was an open secret that those slaves lived the lives of free people.

In short, the very need to pass laws to keep slavery from self-de-structing piecemeal was further evidence of its economic deficiencies, quite aside from its violations of moral and humani-tarian principles.

Chapter 3

The Economics of Medical Care

Medical care is one of many goods and services that can be provided in a wide variety of ways. At one time, it was common for sick people simply to pay doctors and buy medicine individually with their own money. Today, both the medicines and the medical care are often paid for by third parties—either insurance companies or government agencies, or both, with or without some portion being paid by the individual patient. In some cases, medicines and medical care have both been provided by government at no charge to the patient in Canada and some other countries, as they once were in China under Mao Zedong and in the Soviet Union under Stalin. Other countries have had, and some continue to have, various mixtures of government payment and private payment, with varying elements of voluntary choice by patients and physicians.

Since governments get the resources used for medical care by taking those resources from the general population through taxation, there is no net reduction in the cost of maintaining health or curing sicknesses simply because the money is routed through political institutions and government bureaucracies, rather than being paid directly by patients to doctors. Clearly, however, the widespread popularity of government-financed health care means that many people expect some net benefit from this process.

One reason is that governments typically do not simply pay whatever medical costs happen to be, as determined by supply and demand. Governments impose price controls, in order to try to keep the costs of medical care from absorbing so much of their budgets as to seriously restrict other government functions. Government-paid medical care is thus often an exercise in price control, and it creates situations that have been common for centuries in response to price controls on many other goods and services.

PRICE CONTROLS ON MEDICAL CARE

One of the reasons for the political popularity of price controls in general is that part of their costs are concealed—or, at least, are not visible initially when such laws are passed. Price controls are therefore particularly appealing to those who do not think beyond stage one—which can easily be a majority of the voters. Artificially lower prices, created by government order rather than by supply and demand, encourage more use of goods or services, while discouraging the production of those same goods and services. Increased consumption and reduced production mean a shortage.

Even the visible shortages do not tell the whole story, however. *Quality* deterioration often accompanies reduced production, whether what is being produced is food, housing, or numerous other goods and services whose prices have been kept artificially low by government fiat. Quality declines because the incentives to maintaining quality are lessened by price control. Sellers in general maintain the quality of their products or services for fear of losing customers otherwise. But, when price controls create a situation where the amount demanded is greater than the amount supplied—a shortage—fear of losing customers is no longer as strong an incentive. For example, landlords typically reduce painting and repairs when there is rent control, because there is no need to fear vacancies when there are more tenants looking for apartments than there are apartments available.

Nowhere has quality deterioration been more apparent—or more dangerous—than with price controls on medical care. One way in which the quality of health care deteriorates is in the amount of time that a doctor spends with a patient. This was most dramatically demonstrated in the Soviet Union, which had the most completely government-controlled medical system:

> At the neighborhood clinics where 80% of all patients are treated, the norms call for physicians to see eight patients an hour. That is 7.5 minutes per visit, and Soviet studies show that five minutes of each visit is spent on paper work, a task complicated by chronic short supplies of preprinted forms and the absence of computers.
>
> "Our heads spin from rushing," say Pavel, the silver-haired chief of traumatology at a Moscow clinic, who, like some other Russians interviewed for this article, won't give his last name. A dozen patients with splints and slings sit in a dark corridor awaiting their turn at a 1950s-vintage fluoroscope. "We wind up seeing the same patients several times over," the doctor goes on, "when one thorough examination could have solved the problem if we had the time."

Although the Soviet Union was an extreme example, similar policies have tended to produce similar results in other countries. Under government-paid health care in Japan, patients also have shorter and more numerous visits than patients in the United States. Under a Korean health care system copied from Japan, a study found that "even injections of drugs were often split in half to make two visits necessary," because "the doctor can charge for two office visits and two injection fees." After Canada's Quebec province created its own government health plan back in the 1970s, telephone consultations went down, office visits went up and the time per visit went down. In other words, medical conditions which neither the doctor nor the patient previously thought serious enough to require an office visit, before price controls, now took up more time by both the patient (in travel time) and the doctor (in the office), thereby reducing the time available to people who had more serious conditions.

In general, where the doctor is paid per patient visit, then a series of treatments that might have taken five visits to the doctor's office can now take ten shorter visits—or more. Therefore political leaders can proclaim that price controls have succeeded because the cost per visit is now lower than it was in a free market, even though the total costs of treating a given illness have not declined and—typically—have risen. Skyrocketing costs, far beyond anything projected at the outset, have marked government-controlled health care systems in France, Britain, Canada and elsewhere. Responses to such runaway costs have included abbreviated doctors' visit and hospital stays cut short.

The costs in Britain's government-run medical system have increased sharply, both absolutely and as a percentage of the country's rising Gross Domestic Product. The National Health Service in Britain absorbed just under four percent of the country's GDP in 1960 and rose over the years until it absorbed well over seven percent of a larger GDP by 2000. Nevertheless, the number of doctors per capita in Britain was just half as many as in Germany, where half the hospital beds were still in private hands, despite a large role for government financing there. Quality deterioration is another response to rising medical care costs. According to the British magazine *The Economist*, "patients in other rich countries can get prompt treatment with state-of-the-art technologies in clean rather than dirty wards." Apparently not in Britain, where quality deterioration is part of the hidden cost that does not show up in statistics.

Just as artificially low housing prices have led many people to seek their own separate housing units who would not ordinarily do so, if they had to pay the full costs in a free market, so artificially less expensive—in some countries, free—medical care has led many people with minor medical problems to absorb far more of doctors' time and expensive medicines and treatments than they would if they had to pay the costs themselves. France is an example:

> In every healthy Frenchman hides a sick one dying to be diagnosed, goes a wry French saying. The trouble is that doctors are encouraged to give patients what they want—scans, blood tests, antibiotics, sick leave—for fear of losing their custom and thus earning less. If they don't overload prescriptions to counter every conceivable germ and depressive tendency, patients may shop around until they find a doctor who does.

This is not peculiar to the French people or to medical care. More of anything tends to be demanded at a lower price—and especially when it is free. In Canada as well, a news story pointed out: "Since the system sets no limits on demand, patients seek as much care as they can get, driving up costs." In Britain, a twelve-year-old girl received a breast implant, paid for by the National Health Service. Excessive prescriptions were reported as "routine" under China's government-provided health care and patients there "leave the dispensary with bags, rather than bottles, full of pills." China has subsequently moved away from government-provided medical care.

Not only patients, but doctors as well, have incentives to use medical treatments more extensively when the government pays the bills. Many diseases can be treated in a variety of ways, and how often the most expansive—and expensive—treatments will be used can be affected by who is paying. In October 2002, for example, the FBI seized the records of a San Francisco cardiologist who was accused of doing far more open heart surgeries than were called for by medical criteria, as a means of receiving more income from government payments. One patient who was told by this cardiologist that he needed triple by-pass surgery was told by every other cardiologist he consulted that he needed no such thing.

The normal weighing of costs against benefits, which causes more urgent things to be done ahead of less important things when prices ration scarce resources, is less effective when costs are paid by someone other than the actual decision-makers. This can lead to less important things receiving medical attention while urgent things get neglected. When patients pay for their own medical treatments, they are more apt to establish priorities, so that someone with a fractured leg is far more likely to go to doctor than someone with a minor headache. But, when both are treated free of charge to the patient, then people with minor ailments may take up so much of doctors' time and medical resources that those with more serious medical conditions must be forced to wait.

When prices no longer ration, then something else has to ration, since the underlying scarcity does not go away because the government controls prices or provides things free of charge. One of the alternative ways of rationing is by waiting. In 2001, more than 10,000 people in Britain had waited more than 15 months for surgery. This is one of the ways in which the quality of goods and services deteriorate under price controls. Waiting for medical care is particularly costly in human terms, not only because of the needless pain that may be suffered while waiting, but also because the underlying malady may be getting worse when the waiting is not simply a matter of hours spent in a hospital's reception room but months or even years spent on a waiting list before being able to get treatment. People can die from conditions that were initially not very serious, but which grew progressively worse while they were on waiting lists to receive medical care. A celebrated example in Britain involved a woman whose cancer surgery was repeatedly postponed until it had to be cancelled, because the cancer had become inoperable in the course of all the delays. To call this quality deterioration is, if anything, an understatement.

Another feature of price controls which applies with special poignancy to medical care is the black market, which flourished in China under government-supplied medical care:

> Rather than wait in long lines for indifferent treatment, affluent Chinese traditionally "go through the back door" for better service, asking friends to provide an introduction to a doctor or giving gifts or payments to physicians and nurses. This practice, though illegal, can ensure faster, better and friendlier treatment. Mid-level hospital administrators tend to benefit most from this arrangement, as they become engaged in the lucrative practice of providing access to doctors.

A study found similar illegal payments in Japan, where "a $1,000 to $3,000 'gift' to the attending physician is common at top Tokyo hospitals." Official statistics do not capture these illegal financial costs, much less the even more important human costs of hasty diagnosis and treatments in abbreviated visits to doctors' offices and the long time on waiting lists before even reaching a medical facility. Thus, in terms of publicly visible costs and benefits, a price-controlled medical system may be a political success. For years, the Soviet Union boasted of having the largest number of doctors and hospital beds of any country in the world—all the while concealing the fact that it also had rising rates of infant mortality and a declining life expectancy in its population as a whole, facts which came out only in its last years under Mikhail Gorbachev's policy of *glasnost* or openness.

The unrecorded human costs of price-controlled medical care are indirectly indicated by those who opt out. These include patients, doctors, and medical facilities. Patients in countries with government-controlled medical prices have left the overcrowded government sector to seek private treatment at their own expense, either at home or in other countries. It is common for Canadians to go to the United States for medical treatment, but rare for Americans to go to Canada for such treatment. Doctors have also opted out in various ways. Some have gone into private practice, despite laws which make it illegal for them to do so if they treat any patients at all who are enrolled in government plans. Some Health Maintenance Organizations in the United States have stopped accepting certain categories of patients for whom the government's reimbursement is inadequate to cover their costs. Sometimes the opting out occurs earlier, when fewer people enter medical school after the rewards of being a doctor are reduced. More than half the doctors in Britain, for example, were not trained in British medical schools but have been imported from many other countries, including Third World countries where the training may not be up to the standards of British medical schools.

Paying less and getting less—whether less is defined quantitatively or qualitatively—is no bargain, least of all in the case of medical care.

THIRD-PARTY PAYMENTS

Even in the absence of the price-control factor, having medicines or medical care paid for by third parties changes the way individuals use medical care. Despite a tendency to regard medical care as a more or less fixed "need," the amount that is demanded can vary greatly according to who is paying. For example, the use of tax-free medical savings accounts in the United States has tended to increase greatly in December, since unexpended money in those accounts is not carried over to the next year. One chain of eyeglass stores reports that its sales are 25 percent higher in December than in any other month "as people scoop up a second or third pair of fashionable frames." As one such customer, who already had eight or nine pairs of glasses, put it, "They go out of style after a while."

Even if it is medically necessary for a given person to wear glasses, is keeping up with fashions also medically necessary? More to the point, would this same customer have bought eight or nine pairs of glasses with her own money? If not, then medical savings accounts have led to a misallocation of resources to buy things that are not worth what they cost, but which are purchased anyway because the government is helping to pay for them by exempting from taxes the income that goes into medical savings accounts. Eye glasses are not the only goods or services that can be charged to these accounts. Condoms, birth control pills, and massages have also been paid out of medical savings accounts. So long as a physician signs off on the expenditure, it is legal—and the physician has no strong incentives to hold back on the spending of someone else's money.

Free market prices, paid by the customer, do not simply convey more or less inevitable costs. They restrain costs by providing incentives for the individual to use a given good or service only to the extent that its incremental value to that individual is greater than its incremental costs. But, when third parties cover all or part of these costs, then additional increments continue to be used beyond that point. Often a given medical problem can be treated in more than one way. For example, an arthritic knee may be treated by taking medication, having therapeutic exercises, or undergoing surgery. Eyesight problems can be treated not only with glasses of varying degrees of fashion, but also with the use of contact lenses, eye exercises, or laser surgery. Choices among these and other treatments depend not only on how serious the medical problem is, but also on how much each of these treatments costs—and who pays those costs. When third parties pay, the more expensive treatments become more likely than when the individual pays.

Because health care is so often discussed in politics and in media as if there is a more or less fixed amount of "need" and the only question is how to pay for it, much attention has been focused on those who do not have any form of health insurance. But these financial arrangements are not ends in themselves. The real question is: How much medical care is available, whether or not particular individuals have health insurance?

The most poverty-stricken person living on the streets will be treated in an emergency room, with or without health insurance. Abandoned babies are likewise treated without regard to their ability to pay. No doubt those with insurance, and still more so those with wealth of their own, can get more comfortable accommodations in a hospital and can afford more elective or even cosmetic, medical procedures. But to discuss people without health insurance as if they were also without access to medical care is very misleading.

Some uninsured people have low incomes but others with incomes sufficient to purchase health insurance simply choose to use their money for other things, especially when they are young and feel less at risk of medical problems. Forty percent of uninsured Americans are under the age of 25 and more than 60 percent are under the age of 35. Fewer than 10 percent of people over 55 are uninsured, despite the widespread political use of an image of old people who have to choose between food and medical care. That may be the image of the uninsured, but it is hardly the reality.

MEDICAL MALPRACTICE

One of the major costs of American medical care is malpractice insurance for doctors and hospitals. The average cost of this insurance for individual doctors ranges from about $14,000 a year in California to nearly $40,000 a year in West Virginia. In particular specialties, such as obstetrics, the cost of malpractice insurance can exceed $100,000 a year. These costs of course get passed on to patients, the government, or whoever is paying for medical treatments. One-stage thinking has much to do with these costs and with the consequences that follow.

The threat of lawsuits can impose costs on obstetricians which raise their insurance premiums high enough to cause many of these doctors to stop delivering babies, or to stop delivering them in places where high jury awards on dubious evidence make it uneconomic to continue practicing obstetrics. The net result of this can be that pregnant women in those places are at more risk than before because there may be no doctor available in the vicinity to deliver their baby when the time comes.

Ideally, juries would award malpractice damages only when the probability that malpractice had taken place was sufficiently certain, and the award only at a level sufficient to compensate real damages and deter such malpractice in the future. In reality, an injured, deformed, or brain-damaged baby and an eloquent lawyer can lead to jury awards in the millions of dollars, even when it is by no means certain that the doctor who delivered that baby was in any way at fault. A large study conducted jointly by the American College of Obstetricians and Gynecologists and the American Academy of Pediatrics—released in 2003 and reviewed and approved by leading medical authorities in and out of government, as well from as far away as Australia and New Zealand—concluded that "the vast majority of brain damage and cerebral palsy

originates in factors largely or completely *outside* the control of de-
livery-room personnel."

Whether that will stop multimillion dollar jury awards in such
cases is another question. After all, it costs the jury nothing to
"send a message" warning doctors to be more careful, and the particular doctor in the case at hand probably has insurance from a
company that can pay a few million dollars easily out of its billions
of dollars in assets. Only if the jurors think beyond stage one will
they take into account the future costs to pregnant women unable
to find obstetricians in their area at the time of delivery and the
lifelong costs to babies who may incur more or worse injuries or
disabilities as a result. This is especially likely to be the end result
in states where juries hand out multimillion-dollar awards readily,
such as Nevada:

> Kimberly Maugaotega of Las Vegas is 13 weeks pregnant and hasn't
> seen an obstetrician. When she learned that she was expecting, the
> 33-year-old mother of two called the doctor who delivered her sec-
> ond child but was told he wasn't taking any new pregnant patients.
> Dr. Shelby Wilbourn plans to leave Nevada because of soaring med-
> ical malpractice insurance rates there. Ms. Maugaotega says she
> called 28 obstetricians but couldn't find one who would take her.

This is just one of the ways that huge jury awards and the huge
malpractice insurance premiums that result from them increase the
costs of medical care. Another cost is the cost of "defensive
medicine"—medically unnecessary treatments which protect the
doctor from lawsuits, even if they do not protect the patient from
any real danger. For example, because some lawsuits have alleged
that cerebral palsy in newborn babies might have been avoided if
the physician had delivered the baby by Caesarean-section, the
number of Caesarean-section births has been rising to become
one-fourth of all births. This has not reduced the incidence of

cerebral palsy in newborn babies, though it may have reduced the ease of suing doctors. The median award for negligence in childbirth exceeds two million dollars.

As in so many cases, political "solutions" to the malpractice problem can create new problems. One popular political solution has been to put upper limits on the amount of awards for "pain and suffering." But if the carelessness or incompetence of some physician or surgeon has in fact caused someone to be in pain for the rest of his or her life, a quarter of a million dollar cap, as in California, is completely inadequate compensation. The fundamental problem is not with the huge amounts of money awarded, as such, but with the fact that there may be no adequate basis for any award at all. Doctors and hospitals win a majority of the malpractice cases that go to trial but the risk of damage awards in the tens of millions of dollars cause them to settle many cases out of court.

PHARMACEUTICAL DRUGS

While the process of creating a new pharmaceutical drug involves science, it also involves trial and error, often taking years. In the pharmaceutical drug industry, creating a new medicine to cure a particular disease can involve many failures before finally developing a drug that is simultaneously effective, affordable, and without major adverse side-effects for most people. In 2003, an official of the drug producer Pfizer said: "Last year we made over 5,000 compounds. Only half a dozen of them will make it to clinical trials." How many of those half dozen would prove to be successful in the clinical trials and then make it through the approval process of the Food and Drug Administration only the future would tell.

If the pharmaceutical company has spent years working on many different chemical compounds before finally coming up with one that meets all the criteria—and gets the approval of the

Food and Drug Administration as well—then its profits on the successful drug has to cover all its costs on the many unsuccessful ones. Otherwise there will not be sufficient earnings to repay all the individuals, pension funds, and other investors whose money they use to finance the creation of new drugs.

Since the creation of a single new drug typically costs hundreds of million dollars,[1] keeping enough investors willing to supply such huge sums of money is essential to keeping the discovery of new drugs going.

Those who do not think beyond stage one see the situation in wholly different terms. Rather than examine what happens before and after a new drug is created, they essentially treat existing drugs as having been created *somehow* and focus on how these drugs are priced, what profits they earn, and how those prices can be brought down. Since the costs of manufacturing a pharmaceutical drug is often a small fraction of its total costs or of the price paid by the consumer, there are ample opportunities for politicians, journalists, and others to decry the "unconscionable," "outrageous" or "obscene" profits made by charging two dollars a pill when the ingredients in the pill cost only a quarter.

By ingredients they mean physical ingredients, which are usually inexpensive, rather than the knowledge ingredient which is usually astronomically expensive because of years of research, including much trial and error. The same misconception of costs can appear in another form when politicians, journalists, etc., contrast the high price charged for a pharmaceutical drug by the company that created it versus the much lower price of a "generic equivalent" produced by another company, which simply uses the

---

[1]"It can take fifteen years and hundreds of millions of dollars to go from finding a bacterial target to putting a drug into production." James Surowiecki, "No Profit, No Cure," *The New Yorker*, November 11, 2001. "Estimates range from around $250 per drug to more than $800 Million." "Drug Prices: A Much-Needed Primer," *Wall Street Journal*, July 22, 2002, p. A15.

same formula free of charge after the patent has expired. The second company's costs are just the low costs of manufacturing the drug, so that they may be able to make a profit selling a generic equivalent for a fraction of what the company that created the drug charged. In the case of a pill whose ingredients cost a quarter, the generic manufacturer may be able to make a profit charging thirty-five cents for the same pill, causing the brand-name manufacturer who created the drug to be accused of unconscionably exploiting people who are ill and desperate.

The combination of very high fixed costs for developing a new drug and very low incremental costs of producing it leads to other economic consequences that are easy to misunderstand or misrepresent by those who do not think beyond stage one. For example, Canadians pay much lower prices for American pharmaceutical drugs than Americans do. When the Canadian government, which buys vast quantities of medicines for its comprehensive, national government-run health care system, offers an American pharmaceutical company a price which covers the incremental costs of manufacturing a particular drug, but not the vast costs of developing that drug in the first place, the pharmaceutical company's alternatives are (1) to lose millions of dollars in sales by not accepting the offer or (2) earn whatever money it can by accepting the offer, since the past costs have already been paid and are irrelevant to current decision-making. As economists say, "sunk costs are sunk."

While past costs are irrelevant to present decision-making—they are history but they are not economics—those past costs do matter for future decision-making, when pharmaceutical companies decide whether, or to what extent, to invest in developing more new drugs. If those past costs have not been covered, future costs may not be as readily incurred to create future drugs to cure or prevent such scourges as Alzheimer's, AIDS, or cancer.

One of the irrelevant distractions in many discussions of the costs of creating new medications is that much of the drug companies' research is a continuation of more fundamental scientific research done in academic institutions and government agencies such as the National Institutes of Health. Critics who say "the pharmaceutical industry has so far devoted most of its R & D resources not to scientific discovery but to the practical application of discoveries generated at taxpayer expense" are saying much less than meets the eye. In every aspect of our lives, we all stand on the shoulders of giants, and all those giants were not in the past.

The principles of aerodynamics were not discovered by the Wright brothers. They were simply the first people to get a plane off the ground. If no one had ever gotten a plane off the ground, then the principles of aerodynamics would be just an irrelevant curiosity. Similarly, the scientific bases of the numerous inventions by Thomas Edison were not discovered by Edison himself. But we rightly celebrate the work of those who turned known facts and principles into something that could actually be used to make life better. There is similarly no reason to deny the achievements of those who turned others' more fundamental scientific work into something that could make life last longer and be lived with more health and vigor in old age.

The costs incurred in turning scientific discoveries into new medications are no less real and no less important because other individuals and organizations incurred other costs earlier. Nor does the fact that the taxpayers' money was used mean that the best way to make decisions about pharmaceutical drugs is to take those decisions out of the marketplace and have them made by politicians. Yet this non sequitur is what seems to be implied by those who think that the prior costs of scientific discoveries change the economic requirements for producing new medicines.

Those in politics or in the media who do not think beyond stage one may see in government control a means of bringing down the prices of existing medicines, without thinking through whether this will also bring down the rate of discovery of new medicines. However, these efforts at bringing down prices through collective action are usually successful in the short run. That is because seldom is a given medicine the only one that can be used in treating a given disease, so a drug company's ability to hold out against the Canadian or other governments is very limited, when those governments can buy someone else's medications if they do not get the price they want from a particular pharmaceutical company. Moreover, in a country with a government-controlled comprehensive medical care system, there may be little or no market for a given medicine from the small, or non-existent, private sector.

Even in the United States, there are large buyers of pharmaceutical drugs such as health maintenance organizations and the federal government, who can likewise present a pharmaceutical company with a take-it-or-leave-it offer at a price that allows the company to make some money over and above manufacturing costs, but not nearly enough to cover the high fixed costs required to develop new drugs.

To those who do not consider the economics of this process—and that includes not only most of the public, but also politicians, journalists, and others—it can easily appear that the issue is simply one of getting lower prices and the case for government-imposed price controls may seem not only obvious but imperative. In fact, price controls on pharmaceutical drugs have been common in countries around the world, with the United States being a notable exception. The United States is also a notable exception in that a wholly disproportionate share of all the new life-saving drugs in the world are developed in the United States. But few in politics or the media see the connection between these two facts, even though price controls on many other things have reduced the amounts supplied. Yet, even within the United States, there have always been demands for imposing price controls on American pharmaceutical companies as well.

Those who do not think beyond stage one focus on the money that can be "saved" by allowing Canadians to re-export back to the United States the American drugs they have bought at lower prices than Americans pay, thereby reducing the costs of medical care for the American government, individuals and medical organizations. Not only would there be direct savings by individuals and organizations importing American medicines from Canada, the pharmaceutical drug companies would then be under pressure to lower the prices they charge in the United States as well, after losing sales because of competition from the sales of their own medicines being imported from Canada. None of this, however, deals with the crucial question for those who do think beyond stage one: Since the fixed costs have to be paid by somebody, if the development of new medicines is to continue, how can evasions of such payments of fixed costs fail to reduce the rate of investment and discovery of new medicines?

It is not simply a theoretical question. The facts tell the same story. Not all countries have the strong patent protection system that the United States has, which enables American drug companies to have a period of monopoly in which to recover huge fixed costs before the patent expires. Making generic copies of drugs developed by others is easier in countries without strong patent laws, and consequently the prices of these generic copies are typically much lower in such countries than in the United States. But the development of new drugs is also correspondingly much lower, or non-existent, in countries where there is less likelihood of being able to recover fixed costs because generic equivalents keep the prices down.

Policies or legislation prescribing the substitution of generic pharmaceutical drugs for similar or identical brand-name drugs can often reduce the cost to hospitals or health-insurance systems.

Some demand that all drugs be generic, ending the high prices and presumably unconscionable profits of the brand-name drug producers. But here we must beware of the fallacy of composition. What is true for some cannot necessarily be made true for all. The overlooked factor is that generic drug producers are essentially getting a free ride on the costs and experience built up at great expense by producers of brand-name drugs. Those costs cannot be made to disappear by government fiat or by the organized pressure of hospitals and health-insurance companies, even when these entities can force down the prices on drugs that have already been developed. Reducing the brand-name drug producers' ability to recoup their costs means reducing the incentives for continuing the development of *new* drugs to deal with other diseases and conditions.

Sometimes the claim is made that the costs incurred by pharmaceutical manufacturers are mostly for advertising, not research. But, however easy it may be for outside observers to dismiss advertising as an expense that accomplishes nothing for society and only increases the advertiser's profits, that is in fact not the case. The most wonderful drug ever created will help no one's medical condition unless it becomes known. Advertising does that. Nor is making the drug known something that can be done once and for all, and advertising discontinued thereafter, without consequences.

After the patent for the drug Ceclor expired and its producer, Eli Lilly & Co., cut back on the promotion of it when generic substitutes began to be marketed by other companies, prescriptions for this drug fell to one-fifth of the former level, because the generic producers had little or no incentive to advertise, since no one of them would have a large enough share of the increased sales to recover the advertising expenditures. As far as the practical effect on patients is concerned, advertising is as much of an ingredient in the drug's benefits as any of the pharmaceutical components themselves.

There is another aspect to advertising that is seldom understood. When a medication is approved by the Food and Drug Administration for one use and other uses are later discovered for it, the FDA can forbid the pharmaceutical company from advertising the other uses unless and until it has gone through the long and costly process of meeting FDA requirements for that new use. Depending on whether the anticipated additional sales would cover these additional costs—which can run into many millions of dollars—the company may or may not try to get the approval needed to permit advertising uses which medical science has already shown to be beneficial. A classic example is aspirin, which has long been approved as medication for headaches but may be even more valuable in other uses, which it has until recent years been forbidden to advertise:

> There is substantial medical evidence that taking a dose of aspirin can reduce the risk of heart attack in middle-aged males . . . by almost 50 percent. Indeed, the results are so well known that there exists a pamphlet, *Amazing Aspirin*, available for 89¢ at the checkout stand of grocery stores, which discusses this benefit at great length. What is surprising is that neither the package for the aspirin itself nor any advertising for it indicates that valuable use. Why does Bayer largely forego the possibility of the increased sales from providing this information to consumers?
>
> On March 2, 1988, at a meeting in the offices of FDA Commissioner Frank Young, all companies making aspirin were told that they could not advertise the benefits of the product in reducing risks for first heart attacks. If they did, the FDA would bring legal action.

As a consequence, "the ban on aspirin advertising undoubtedly causes tens of thousands of needless deaths per year." Obviously, the Food and Drug Administration's ban on advertising medication for purposes that the FDA has not approved is designed to promote safety. But the purpose of the ban does not change the consequences. Fortunately, in this case, the FDA eventually relented and allowed aspirin companies to advertise the use of their product to reduce deaths from heart attacks. However, the deaths of those who might have saved their lives by taking aspirin, if they had known about its benefits for those suffering heart attacks, was a high price paid for the delay.

More fundamentally, when thousands of lives can be saved by advertising, are those lives any less important than a similar number of lives saved by the development of an entirely new medication? Yet many treat it as a condemnation of pharmaceutical drug companies that they spend so much on advertising. What research does for the scientific community—provide information they might otherwise not know—is what advertising does for doctors and patients. Moreover, because physicians are the ones who prescribe pharmaceutical drugs, they are a more knowledgeable audience than the audiences for many other kinds of advertising, and are therefore harder to deceive or to impress with mere puffery. Moreover, a drug company which attempted to deceive doctors about a particular drug would be risking an enormously costly loss of confidence in that company by doctors who prescribe a wide range of medicines, and who could therefore steer billions of dollars in expenditures away from the deceiving company and toward its rivals.

The drug approval process attempts to reduce the risks of new and untried medicines before they are made available to the general public. In addition to being reasonably safe for most people, pharmaceutical drugs must also be shown to be effective for whatever medical conditions they are intended to treat. A medicine that is safe but ineffective is not only a fraud but a danger, as it may be used for diseases and conditions for which there are alternative treatments that are in fact effective, thereby depriving sick people of benefits that are already available. Yet the question of *how safe* and *how effective*, at what cost, must be considered as regards the years of tests and trials prescribed by the FDA's drug approval process.

The more years that the trials go on and the larger the number of people in the sample taking the drug, the more reliable the end results as to both safety and effectiveness—and the more sick people will be left to suffer and perhaps die while these processes go on. A new drug may be tested for effectiveness against a placebo or against the effectiveness of some other drug. The latter may be a better process in terms of the validity of the end results but one such trial involving more than 30,000 people added *another eight years* to the testing process. A lot of people can die in eight years— and yet absolute certainty is still not achievable by human beings, no matter how much testing goes on. Moreover, these deaths during the trial period are not necessarily recouped over the lifetime of the particular drug or treatment, which may be superseded by new drugs or treatments for the same diseases in few or many years, as the case may turn out to be.

The incentives and constraints facing government officials in charge of testing pharmaceutical drugs are asymmetrical. Ideally, these officials could weigh the costs and the benefits equally—for example, stopping the testing process at the point where the estimated number of lives lost while waiting longer for more drug tests to be completed would exceed the estimated number of lives saved by getting more data on the drug's safety. But neither the public, the media, nor the political leaders to whom health officials are ultimately responsible are likely to use that standard.

If a thousand children die from a new drug allowed into the market with less testing and ten thousand would die while more testing was going on, the public outcry over the deaths of those thousand children would bring the wrath of the whole political system down on the heads of those officials who permitted the drug to be approved with "inadequate" testing. But if ten or a hundred times as many people die while prolonged testing goes on, there will be few, if any, stories about those people in the media.

For one thing, the thousand deaths attributable to the drug approved by the FDA are far more likely to be provable deaths to identifiable individuals, whose stories can make headlines, than deaths to ten thousand unidentifiable individuals whose inability to get a life-saving drug shows up only in death-rate statistics comparing what happens where the drug is available and where it is not available. But statistics are never as dramatic as television interviews with distraught widows or mothers of those have who died from the side effects of a drug.

These asymmetrical incentives and constraints have led American health officials to ban life-saving drugs that have been in use for years, if not decades, in Europe—with few, if any, ill effects—because these drugs have not yet gone through the long and costly process necessary to get approval under American laws and policies. Even if the effectiveness and relative safety of these drugs have been reported in scientific studies published in leading medical journals, that is not accepted as a substitute for the prescribed FDA approval process. Desperately ill people have been known to either have the medicines smuggled into the country or, if they can afford it, go outside the United States themselves to get them. Sometimes safety precautions can be carried to the point where they are fatal.

IMPLICATIONS

At the heart of the problems created by price controls on medical care and attempts to keep down the prices of pharmaceutical drugs is the belief that prices are just nuisances to be circumvented. In reality, prices convey an underlying reality that is not nearly as easily changed as the prices are.

The costs of unnecessary Caesarean-section births do not go away because of price controls. Moreover, these costs are not simply money costs. Many of the costs in medical care are costs paid in pain and deaths, rather than in money. These costs are not going to be lower, but higher, when attempts to avoid paying the huge costs of developing pharmaceutical drugs lead to a reduced creation of such drugs. We need not wait to see this process unfold in the United States because we already see that countries which have succumbed to the politically attractive policy of keeping drug prices low by fiat, or by ineffective patent protection, have much lower rates of discovery of major new medications than does the United States. The costs to a pregnant woman and her baby of not being able to find an obstetrician, or to find one in time, can be a lifetime of coping with unnecessary birth defects.

Various organized groups in a position to bargain for lower medical charges or lower drug prices—government agencies, health insurance companies, or large health maintenance organizations, for example—may receive preferential prices but the total costs do not go away and have to be paid by somebody. One consequence is a multi-tiered set of prices for the same medical treatment or the same medication, with the highest prices of all being paid by patients who do not have health insurance, do not belong to a health maintenance group, and are not covered by any government program. Thus a given medical procedure at the UCLA Medical Center, for which Medicaid pays $127, is priced at $90 when covered by Medicare, up to $242 when covered by health maintenance organizations, and $460 when paid by individuals without insurance and who are not part of any of these plans.

In short, misconceptions of the economic function of prices lead not only to price controls, with all their counterproductive consequences, but also to organized attempts by various institutions, laws, and policies to get those prices paid for by somebody else. For society as a whole, there is no somebody else. Yet few of those in politics seem prepared to face that fact. Economists may say that there is no such thing as a free lunch but politicians get elected by promising free lunches.

Most of what are called attempts to "bring down the cost of medical care" are not that at all. They are attempts to bring down the *prices* charged by physicians, hospitals, and pharmaceutical companies. Many of those who are most active in trying to bring down these prices are most resistant to bringing down the real costs of medical care by such things as making it harder for lawyers to win frivolous lawsuits against doctors and hospitals or making the Food and Drug Administration's approval process for new medicines less time-consuming, or reducing the layers of bureaucracy administering various schemes of third-party payments. These things all drain resources that could otherwise be used to treat or cure diseases, or to prevent them.

The negative consequences of price controls on medical care seen in various countries around the world are not just incidental mistakes that can be corrected by tweaking the health care system. They are the medical version of patterns seen in response to price controls on many sorts of goods and services, over a period of centuries. Four things have almost invariably followed the imposition of controls to keep prices below the level they would reach under supply and demand in a free market: (1) increased use of the product or service whose price is controlled, (2) reduced supply of the same product or service, (3) quality deterioration, and (4) black markets. All these things have been found when the prices of medical care have been controlled—and all are particularly harmful in matters involving pain, disability, and death.

Increased use of the medical system by some leaves less time and resources for others. The time taken up in a physician's office by people whose minor problems would be handled by a brief phone call to the doctor, or perhaps with just a chat with a pharmacist, if they were spending their own money, means less time available at the doctor's office for others afflicted with more serious illnesses. Time spent by surgeons performing operations that are not medically necessary, but which they may consider to be legally necessary to protect themselves against ruinous lawsuits, is time that is not available to perform surgeries that may be very necessary for others, for whom delay is not just an inconvenience but a matter of needlessly prolonged suffering and increasing dangers from conditions that are worsening as time passes.

Reduced supply in the wake of short-sighted laws and policies that focus on price include not only a reduced rate of discovery of new cures and preventive vaccines, but also a reduced supply of doctors as the growing hassles of bureaucracy and the growing hazards of unfounded malpractice lawsuits lead some existing doctors to retire earlier than they might under less stressful conditions, and a lesser attraction to medical careers by some young people who find all the imposed requirements, restrictions, and hypocrisies to be things they would rather avoid by going into other fields. But these and other hidden costs, to doctors and patients alike, are unlikely to affect those who do not think beyond stage one when considering laws and policies.

Perhaps the most poisonous effect of attempts to promote political control of medical care and to extract multi-million dollar damage awards in malpractice lawsuits has been a demonizing of the very people who have extended our lives and made those lives more healthful and vigorous than was ever common before among elderly people. Doctors and the producers of modern pharmaceutical drugs have been rhetorically transformed into villains by those who would present themselves as our rescuers in politics or in the courtrooms. There is no need to exempt either doctors or drug companies from criticism, where it is deserved, but neither should our would-be political or legal saviors be exempt from criticism.

Whatever policy solutions may be sought for various medical problems should begin with a focus on the underlying realities, not the rhetoric, the images, or the prices that appear on the surface.

Chapter 4

The Economics of Housing

Housing costs are a major item in most people's budgets. For those who own their own homes, the value of the house is often the largest item in their inventory of personal wealth. Whether housing costs are high or low affects what kind of standard of living individuals and families can afford with what is left over after paying for a place to live. The old rule of thumb that housing should cost about one-fourth of one's income has become outdated for 28 million Americans, who pay upwards of 30 percent of their incomes for housing. In some places, it is not uncommon for people to pay half their monthly income for the rent on their apartments. Clearly that restricts what kind of lifestyle they can afford with the other half.

Despite a widespread recognition of the problem of high real estate costs in some places, the nature and causes of that problem have often been distorted, and much of the hand-wringing about a lack of "affordable housing" has been done by people who are themselves a major reason for sky-high housing prices. The political presentation of the problem differs greatly from an economic analysis of it.

The price of housing varies according to many things. One is the quality of the housing itself. Mansions generally cost more than bungalows, though there are places where a bungalow costs more than it would cost to buy a mansion in some other places.

When we say that housing prices are higher in one community than in another, we implicitly mean housing of a given quality. Prices mean little if we are comparing apples and oranges—say, a villa on the beach versus a cabin in the woods.

Many social, as well as economic, problems revolve around housing. Homelessness is one of the most painfully visible. In some communities, very high rents and housing prices force many individuals and families into very difficult choices. Both parents may have to work and put their children into day care facilities all day. Some couples may be unable to afford to have children at all because they can barely afford housing, even if one or both work an extra job. Others, who simply cannot come up with the money for even a modest home or apartment in communities with exorbitant housing prices, may have to live some distance away and spend two or three hours a day commuting to and from their jobs. Two or more families may crowd into a small house or apartment designed for one family. Savings may be depleted in an effort to make ends meet. As bad as such situations are, sometimes popular political "solutions" can make things even worse.

Before considering any solutions, we need to understand what the problem is and what the alternatives are. Why are prices for similar housing so radically different in different communities? Any number of factors might be responsible but the real question is: What does the empirical evidence suggest? Given those particular factors, what needs to be done—or undone?

Prices are not the only concern when it comes to housing. The quality of the housing matters, not just to those who live in it but also to others who can be affected by the appearance of neighboring houses, and by whether their decay or neglect threatens to lower the value of their own homes. Sometimes quality includes a particular character that a particular community cherishes, either in the style of its houses or the kinds of people who live in the community. How far can the existing community's desires go, without taking into account what other individual residents and potential residents might prefer? What about rent control, land restrictions, property rights, housing segregation, slum clearance and building codes? These complex factors need to be examined one by one.

HOUSING PRICES

During the same week, an impressive-looking four-bedroom, six-bath house with 4,370 square feet of space and "a screen-enclosed pool/spa," located adjacent to a golf course and country club, was advertised in the *Wall Street Journal* for $550,000, while a rather ordinary-looking house on an ordinary city street with just 1,300 square feet of space and no pool, was advertised in the *Palo Alto Weekly* for $1,095,000. The first house was located in Leesburg, Florida, while the house costing nearly twice as much was located in Palo Alto, California, near Stanford University. Meanwhile, a house with 6,000 square feet of space, including an indoor lap pool, and set on more than an acre of land in Elmira, New York, was advertised for $349,000. A number of less grandiose houses in Elmira were advertised for less than $100,000, even though most were larger and at least as attractive as the house in Palo Alto that was advertised for more than a million dollars.

Why were houses selling for more than ten times as much in one community as in another? Clearly, it does not cost ten times as much to build a house in one place as in another. Construction costs seldom, if ever, vary by such magnitudes. Realtors sometimes explain such disparities by saying that the three most important factors in housing prices are "location, location, and location." In a sense, that is true. But, in another sense, that explanation can be very misleading. The houses in Leesburg and Elmira had more at-

tractive individual locations than the one in Palo Alto, in addition
to being more attractive houses in themselves. Nevertheless, location is important in the sense that undoubtedly most houses in
Palo Alto cost far more than most houses in Leesburg or Elmira.
But that fact is not an explanation. In reality, it calls for an explanation itself.

Housing prices may be higher in one place than in another for
any of a wide range of reasons. The growth of industry, income,
or population may be greater in one place, leading to more competition for given amounts of land or housing. In addition to
these or other effects on the demand for housing, there are effects on the supply side of the equation. Restrictions on the use
of land or on the building of housing can cause rising prices of
homes or apartments.

In the case of Palo Alto, the prices of homes nearly quadrupled in
one decade—the 1970s—while the population actually declined
and several schools had to be closed, as the number of children enrolled fell by a third. For California as a whole, that same decade
saw its housing prices rise dramatically above those in the rest of
the country, even though the rate of increase in income in California was *less* than that in the country as a whole. This strongly suggests that the cause of rising housing prices in California was not
from the demand side but from the supply side. The average home
price nationwide was $153,000 in 2002, while the average on the
San Francisco peninsula —the area including the city and stretching southward to Silicon Valley, 30 miles away—was $500,000. By
and large, these prices more than three times the national average
were not due to grander houses on the San Francisco peninsula, but
to grander prices for ordinary houses. In Palo Alto, not a single new
house was built during the years when home prices skyrocketed.

In the popular political and media vision of the "affordable housing" issue, this is a national problem for which government subsi-

dies are a necessary part of any solution. In reality, it is not a national problem but a highly localized problem in a relatively few places with sky-high rents and astronomical home prices. Moreover, it is seldom the housing, as such, that is expensive. What has an exorbitant price is the land on which the housing sits.

Land Use Restrictions

An empirical study under the auspices of the National Bureau of Economic Research concluded that zoning laws "are highly correlated with high prices" of housing and that severe land use restrictions are confined to a relatively few places, such as New York City or parts of California. In short, it is the land that is very expensive in these places, rather than the houses or apartments built on the land. In most of the country, "housing costs are quite close to the cost of new construction," the NBER study concluded, and these are areas where "land is quite cheap." As an example of how much the land adds to the cost of housing in various places, the NBER study estimated that the value of a quarter-acre lot adds about $140,000 to the price of a house in Chicago, over and above the cost of construction. In San Diego, a quarter-acre lot adds about $285,000 to the cost of the house itself, in New York City the same size lot adds about $350,000, and in San Francisco nearly $700,000.

Naturally, the higher the cost of a given amount of land, the greater the tendency to reduce the amount of land per house. In the case of apartment buildings, the tendency would be to build taller buildings, so as to increase the amount of rental income without increasing the cost of the land on which the building sits. However, the same political tendencies which produce horizontal restrictions on land use can also produce vertical restrictions, limiting how tall buildings can be built, as well as prescribing how much land there must be around each house or apartment build-ing. These two tendencies do not always go together, so that the higher housing prices which both produce may or may not result in homes packed closer together and apartment buildings rising higher and higher. Where the law mandates an acre of land around each house or limits the height of residential buildings to eight stories, for example, housing costs tend to be especially expensive.

Height restrictions on apartment buildings have other conse-quences as well. Obviously, the shorter the buildings, the more of them are required to house a given population. This means that more land will be used, resulting not only in higher rents per apart-ment, but also in a spreading out of the community, sometimes re-ferred to as "urban sprawl," and longer commutes to work. These longer commutes in turn result in more highway accidents, includ-ing fatalities, so that not all the costs are purely monetary. Given the high man-made costs of various restrictions on land use, how and why do such restrictions occur? One reason is that many voters simply do not think beyond stage one—that is, they do not see the connection between land use restrictions and the various conse-quences which unfold over time.

Another reason is that those who clearly do see the connection may not pay those costs themselves, and may even gain financially from laws which cost others dearly, both financially and in terms of a reduced quality of life—or, in some cases, a shortening of life from highway accidents. Those who already own their own homes will see the value of their homes rise as restrictions are put on the building of new homes. It is those who are already living in a com-munity who vote on its laws, while newcomers are the ones con-fronted with the higher housing prices that these restrictive laws create. Many of the people who are hardest hit are those who can-not afford to live in the community, even if they work there.

The most severe land use restrictions are those which simply forbid the building of any housing at all in specified areas. Such laws are typically described politically in terms of their ostensible goals—"open space"—rather than in terms of what they actually do, which is ban the building of housing and other structures. When more than half the land in San Mateo County, on the San Francisco peninsula, is legally off-limits to housing as "open space," it can hardly be surprising that the price of the remaining land is higher than in places without such severe restrictions on land use. Nor is San Mateo County unique. Such housing ban ("open space") policies are common in communities on the San Francisco peninsula.

History tells the same story as economics. Before such laws and policies spread through much of coastal California in the 1970s, housing prices in that state were very similar to what they were in the rest of the country. Afterwards, California prices for given housing became some multiple of what they were in places without such severe land use restrictions. Indeed, housing prices in coastal California became some multiple of housing prices in that same state's interior valleys, where such policies either did not exist or were far less severe. Particular places in other parts of the country with land use restrictions similar to those in coastal California have likewise had very high prices for homes and very high rents for apartments.

Loudoun County, Virginia, for example, enacted laws in 2001 which restricted the building of homes to one house per 10 acres in some places, 20 acres in others and 50 acres in still others. According to the *Washington Post*: "The board's actions yesterday wiped 83,158 potential homes from Loudoun's plans"—no doubt ensuring rising prices for existing homes. Outsiders who might have lived in those tens of thousands of additional homes of course had no vote in Loudoun County. In an earlier time, their interests might nevertheless have been represented in the marketplace by landowners whose property rights to dispose of their land as they saw fit would have been protected by the courts. Obviously there would be more buyers—and therefore more profits available for those existing landowners who were prepared to sell—when developers were free to determine how many houses they would build per acre than when such decisions are restricted by law.

The crucial point here, however, is not the good or bad fortune of landowners or developers, but the fact that it is the demand of home-seekers—including apartment tenants—which enables developers to profit by supplying that demand. The real contest is between those who wish to buy homes and rent apartments in Loudoun County, on the one hand, versus those current Loudoun County voters who pass laws at no cost to themselves that impose great costs on others. In short, there are two competing sets of people who wish to use the same resources in different ways. Property rights allow this competition to take place in the marketplace, while court-sanctioned abridgements of property rights allow the competition to take place through a political process in which only one set of competitors can vote.

While property rights are often thought of as rights whose purpose and effect are to protect those fortunate enough to own property, the larger purpose is to serve the economic needs of the whole society, including people who own no property. In the case of housing, property rights allow the interests of people who rent apartments to carry weight in economic competition because, although they own no housing and may have modest incomes, in the aggregate their purchasing power can exceed that of affluent residents in a community that wants to keep them out. Intermediaries such as developers bid against the affluent residents on the basis of the money they anticipate making from building and renting apartments. In such a competition, mansions on large estates can be bid away and the land then broken up into smaller units, on which more modest homes and apartment buildings can be built.

Even if many existing residents wish to maintain their community as it is, if individual property rights are respected by the courts, then those particular individuals who find the developers' bids for their property to be irresistible will sell—and the remaining residents will find the character of the community changing around them, whether they resist selling or not. At this point, the holdouts may decide to leave and seek to find the kind of community they like somewhere else. The alternative is to forestall this whole process before it can get under way by abridging individual property rights through collective action to pass land use restrictions under such names as "open space" laws, "environmental protection" policies, or whatever other phrases have political resonance.

Part of this process may include demonizing developers as "selfish" people preoccupied with making money. In reality, developers almost never want to acquire land and build different kinds of housing on it for their own individual use or to indulge their own personal tastes. They are intermediaries whose actions are based on what large numbers of *other* people want and are willing to pay for. To say that the developers want to make money, as everyone must who is not independently wealthy, is to shift the focus from the large numbers of prospective renters and buyers of more modest houses, who are the real competitors bidding against existing affluent residents in a particular area. Nor is it clear that it is less selfish to deny others the same right to choose what kind of housing and community they prefer as one claims for oneself.

Despite the depiction of property rights as mere protections of those who own substantial property, it has often been the affluent and the wealthy who have abridged property rights through the political process, in order to keep working class and other less

affluent people from coming into their communities and changing its character via the developers and the financial institutions
which supply developers with the capital to bid away land from
existing owners. The San Francisco peninsula is just one example
of the kinds of places where this pattern has emerged, beginning
in the 1970s, as courts increasingly countenanced the abrogation
of individual property rights in the name of local political control
of land use. Moreover, land use restrictions in California began to
emerge in community after community with an influx of affluent
and wealthy people into Silicon Valley and their political ascendancy over working class and small business residents in those
communities.

As the development of Silicon Valley brought in more computer
software engineers and high-tech entrepreneurs who made for-
tunes during the computer boom, the political control of local
community after local community changed, as city councils and
appointed environmental commissions came more and more under
the influence or outright control of the newcomers—who then
used these institutions to ensure that other newcomers would not
be able to displace them.

Nor was this simply a matter of majority rule. Often the political
ascendancy of Silicon Valley elites and local academics and students was based on the fact that more educated people voted more
regularly than others, and on the fact that the elections at which
land use issues were voted on were often held in the spring, rather
than in the fall, when general elections for local, state, and national
offices would bring out more of the general public. Thus, one study
concluded, one-fourth of the local population could control the
political outcomes in elections on land use issues. This tended to
be the wealthier and more educated one-fourth, who owned their
own upscale homes, rather than the apartment renters and owners
of more modest houses in these communities.

Similar political processes led to similar results in some other parts of the country. Court rulings which allowed college and university students to vote in local elections, even though their permanent homes were elsewhere, provided political support for land use restrictions under a variety of politically attractive slogans and visions. Since some college towns were in proximity to high-tech industries and the consulting firms and venture capitalists they attracted, such coalitions could often gain control of local political institutions, driving local housing prices far higher than prices in most other parts of the country. That was seldom, if ever, the avowed purposes of such people, which typically revolved around the exaltation of the environment and the demonization of those who would build anything on it. Meanwhile, many of these same advocates of land use restrictions would also proclaim their concern over a need for "affordable housing."

The virtual impossibility of producing much housing that ordinary people could afford under severe land use restrictions led to various token amounts of affordable housing being created, either by government subsidies or by imposing legal requirements on private developers to build housing to be sold or rented "below market," as a precondition for getting permits to build at all. The amount of "affordable housing" produced by either of these methods was of course very limited by the unwillingness of taxpayers to pay for massive amount of subsidies and by the fact that developers could recover their losses on "below market" housing only by increasing still more the rent and home sale prices to others, who obviously did not have unlimited resources either.

The kinds of people adversely affected by land use restrictions and the rise of housing prices they could not afford include many people that every community employs, such as school teachers, nurses, and policemen, but who are seldom paid enough to be able to live in the communities where they work, when those communities have skyrocketing housing costs. For example, a study published in *The Economist* found that the average salary of a nurse would make a two-bedroom apartment affordable, with 30 percent of that salary going for rent, in Dallas, Boston, or Chicago, would almost make it affordable in Washington, but would be less than three-quarters of what would be needed to rent such an apartment in San Francisco.

People with children are doubly affected because, if they are young enough to have small children, they usually have not yet reached their peak earnings years, and having extra mouths to feed reduces whatever resources they might otherwise have available to pay for housing. Less affluent ethnic minorities obviously are particularly affected by very high prices for homes or apartments. All of these groups tend to decline as a share of the population in communities with severe land use restrictions.

The sheriff's department in Redwood City, California, has bought a house, so that its deputies will have a place to sleep after they have worked long hours of overtime. That is because these deputies typically live so far from Redwood City that it would be dangerous for them to drive home tired at night after having worked overtime on some local law enforcement crisis. Various schemes for providing "affordable housing" for teachers have surfaced in a number of communities on the San Francisco peninsula, though these schemes seldom go beyond token numbers of housing units, for the same reasons that "affordable housing" through subsidies are seldom adequate for dealing with the housing problems of other groups.

The black population in San Francisco declined from more than 79,000 in 1990 to less than 61,000 in 2000, even though the city's population as a whole grew by more than 50,000 people. In adjacent San Mateo County, the black population fell from more than 35,000 to less than 25,000 during the same decade, even though the total population of this county also grew by about

50,000 people. The number of children likewise declined in both San Francisco and San Mateo County during the same decade. All the while, people in such places speak of a need for "diversity" and "affordable housing"—neither of which they have or are likely to get, as their populations become whiter and older with rising housing prices.

Population Displacement

What happens to the people who find themselves forced to move out of communities whose rents and home prices they can no longer afford? They move into communities in the surrounding areas—nearby if they can afford it or farther away if they cannot. If their jobs are still in a high-rent city like San Francisco, then they commute, often from considerable distances. In any event, as the exodus from high-rent communities continues, housing prices are then forced up in the communities to which the displaced population moves.

At one time, high housing prices in San Francisco drove many people to relocate across the Bay in Oakland or other parts of Alameda County. But, after a while, this increased demand drove housing prices up in Alameda County to levels that many people there could not afford, and so they moved farther inland to find housing within the range of their incomes. For example, a story in the *San Francisco Chronicle* in 2003 began:

> Each morning at 4:30 am, Frank Montgomery rolls down the driveway of his brand new home to begin the 70-minute trek to work at a Sunol water filtration plant in Alameda County.

Far from being atypical, this commuter represented a growing trend. Data from the U.S. Bureau of the Census showed a 49 percent increase between the 1990 and 2000 censuses, in the number of people commuting from seven outlying counties into the nine counties in and around San Francisco. "Many of them endure hours-long drives on congested highways," according to the *San Francisco Chronicle*. Two of the most distant counties in this group—Santa Cruz County and San Joaquin County—sent more than 26,000 and more than 34,000 people, respectively, on the long commute into the San Francisco Bay area.

Mr. Montgomery was all too typical. He was, incidentally, nevertheless paying $267,000 for the home from which he spent more than an hour each way commuting to work in Alameda County. But that was still much less than what he would have had to pay to live in Alameda County or the other counties bordering San Francisco. While the average price of homes in San Francisco was more than half a million dollars in 2003, it was just over $400,000 in Contra Costa Country, on the other side of Alameda Country, and was below $250,000 in still more distant counties in California's interior valleys. Sales agents out in the valleys report that most of those who are looking for homes in new subdivisions there "are Bay Area residents thrilled by the idea of paying less than $300,000 for a 2,000-square-foot house."

The prices are lower out in California's valleys, not only because they are farther away from San Francisco and the ocean, but also because the restrictions on building are not as severe as they are on the San Francisco peninsula, where anti-growth forces have more political influence. Moreover, the *time* required to get permits to build is usually less in these more conservative areas, where there are not as many anti-growth activist groups to make objections and not as many officials who have to give their objections great weight, in view of their lesser political strength. The old adage "time is money" applies especially in real estate, where millions of dollars are invested in home building that can be brought to a halt while even unfounded complaints about "environmental impact" are investigated. Meanwhile, builders who borrowed these millions have to continue paying interest on all this money, and eventually those costs are recouped in higher apartment rents and higher home prices.

Even in the central valley, however, a rapid growth in population, due to people displaced from in and around San Francisco, has produced a rapid growth in housing prices, though not to the levels found in coastal California. In just five years, the average price of a house out in Merced County—more than a hundred miles from San Francisco—rose from $96,000 to $166,000. One sign of the economic reasons for population displacement is that, while the black populations of San Francisco and San Mateo County have declined significantly in just one decade—as has the black population of Los Angeles, Marin County, Monterey, and other coastal communities—out in the valleys it is the white population which is expected to be overtaken soon by the various minorities moving in, and to become a minority themselves.

Rent Control

One solution to the problem of "affordable housing" that many find attractive is rent control. It shares both economic and political characteristics with other forms of price control. Its political advantage is that its goal is attractive, so that it gains the political support of those who think in terms of desirable goals, rather than in terms of the incentives and constraints created—and the consequences of such incentives and constraints. Those who do not think beyond stage one find rent control especially attractive because the good effects come immediately, while the bad effects come later—and persist for decades.

Among the consequences of price controls in general have been (1) a shortage, as the quantity demanded increases and the quan-

tity supplied decreases, both in response to artificially lower prices,
(2) a decline in quality, as the shortage makes it unnecessary for
the sellers to maintain high quality in order to sell, (3) a black market, when the difference between the legal price and the price people are willing to pay becomes large enough to compensate for the
risks of breaking the law. These same consequences have recurred
again and again, for all sorts of different goods and services whose
prices have been held down by law, in countries around the world,
over a period of centuries, among people of every race, and under
governments ranging from monarchy to democracy to totalitarian
dictatorship. It should hardly be surprising that similar things happen in the housing market when there is rent control.

Perhaps the most basic principle in economics is that people
tend to buy more at a lower price than at a higher price. Rent control enables people to demand more housing than they would
otherwise. In San Francisco, a study in 2001 showed that 49 percent of that city's rent-controlled apartments were occupied by
just one person each. Similar patterns have been found in New
York City and in Sweden. One reason, then, for a housing shortage under rent control laws is that more people occupy more
housing than they would in a competitive market, where they
would have to bid against others whose needs for housing might
be more urgent than theirs or who would have two incomes from
which to bid for housing.

The other reason for a housing shortage is that less housing gets
supplied at a lower price than at a higher price. Builders tend to reduce the amount of housing they build when their ability to recover their costs from the rents they charge is reduced. Where rent
control laws are severe, there may be no new housing built at all,
except for government-subsidized housing where the taxpayers
make up the difference between the cost of supplying housing and
the rents that can be charged under rent control. Therefore one of
the consequences of rent control over time is an increase in the av-

erage age of housing, as the building of new housing declines or stops completely.

A study in San Francisco in 2001 found that more than three-quarters of its rent-controlled housing was more than half a century old and 44 percent of it was more than 70 years old. In Melbourne, Australia, not a single new building was built in the first nine years after World War II because rent control laws made it unprofitable to build any. In Massachusetts, a state law banning local rent control laws led to the building of residential housing in some communities for the first time in a quarter of a century.

Usually, rent control laws do not apply to office buildings, so there may surplus office space, with high vacancy rates, in the same city where there is a housing shortage with virtually no vacancies available in rent-controlled apartment buildings. In some places, rent control laws do not apply to luxury housing, so there is a shift of resources from the building of ordinary housing for ordinary people to the building of luxury housing that only the very affluent or the wealthy can afford. A study of rent control in various countries in Europe concluded: "New investment in unsubsidized rented housing is essentially nonexistent in all the European countries surveyed, except for luxury housing." Such shifts to luxury housing help explain one of the supreme paradoxes of rent control—that cities with rent control laws typically have *higher* rents than cities without such laws. San Francisco, after decades of severe rent control laws, has had the highest apartment rents in the nation, with the rent on two-bedroom apartments averaging more than $2,000 a month.

Not only does rent control reduce incentives to build new housing, it reduces incentives to maintain existing housing. Painting, repairs and other maintenance activities all cost money. In a competitive market, landlords have no choice but to spend that money, in order to attract tenants and keep their apartments filled. Under rent control, however, there are more applicants than apartments, so there is less need to maintain the appearances of the premises or the functioning of the equipment that keeps the heating system and other systems working. In short, existing housing tends to deteriorate faster, as a result of reduced maintenance under rent control, and replacements are built more slowly, if at all. Declining numbers of rental units available after rent control laws were passed have been observed in various American cities, as well as in Canada and overseas.

Where rooms, apartments or houses are rented where the landlord lives, such housing units are particularly likely to be withdrawn from the market when the rent is kept too low to compensate for the inconvenience of having someone else living in the same apartment, or upstairs in a duplex, or in a backyard bungalow. Within three years after rent control was imposed in Toronto in 1976, 23 percent of all rental units in owner-occupied dwellings were withdrawn from the housing market. When rent control in London was extended in 1975 to cover furnished rental units, the number of ads for such units in the *London Evening Standard* fell 75 percent below the number of ads the previous year. All these experiences from various countries tell the same story: People supply less at a lower price, while other people demand more at those lower prices, thereby creating a shortage.

Shortages tend to spawn black markets, where illegal payments are made, in order to get more than is available through legal channels. Bribes to landlords or building superintendents to be put at the top of waiting lists have been one common form of black market activity under rent control. Other forms of illegal activity include landlords' abandonment of buildings after the services they were legally required to provide cost more than the rent they were legally able to collect. The New York City government has found itself in possession of literally thousands of abandoned buildings, as landlords fled underground to escape ruinous losses. Many of these buildings have been boarded up, even though they are perfectly capable of providing much-needed housing, if maintained. The number of housing units in abandoned buildings in New York City is far more than enough to house all the homeless people sleeping on the city's streets.

Although rent control is often thought of as a way to protect the poor from unaffordable housing, only the poor who initially occupied the rent-controlled housing benefit. Those who are on the inside looking out—whether rich or poor—benefit when rent control begins. Later, others on the outside looking in benefit only to the extent that they are relatives or friends of the initial beneficiaries and have the rent-controlled housing passed on to them when the original occupiers leave or die. Some outsiders bribe the original occupiers to get the rent-controlled apartment. In any event, the actual connection between income and the benefits of rent control are tenuous. More than one-fourth of the households in rent-controlled apartments in San Francisco in 2001 had incomes of $100,000 or more.[1]

As with other forms of price control, rent control does not reduce costs. Many rent control advocates are in fact often also advocates of other policies which increase the cost of building and maintaining housing. These include policies mandating various amenities that must accompany housing developments, including bike paths, open space or recreational areas to be used by city residents in general, rather than just by the tenants of the development itself. Providing such amenities can be the price that developers must pay in order to get building permits, but ulti-

---

[1]Incidentally, this was the first empirical study of rent control commissioned by the city of San Francisco. Since rent control began there in 1979, this means that for more than two decades these laws were enforced and extended with no serious attempt to gauge their actual economic and social consequences, as distinguished from their political popularity.

mately it is the tenants in such developments who reimburse the developers by paying higher rents.

Often the same local authorities who impose rent control also impose environmental requirements that are not only costly in themselves, but whose technicalities invite costly lawsuits by those claiming that the requirements have been violated. Restrictions on what building materials will be permitted, how much construction workers must be paid, and other requirements all add to the cost of housing. If rent control does not permit recovery of these costs, then the building of housing can be expected to decline or to stop entirely.

HOUSING "REFORMS"

For more than a century, political and social movements in various countries have promoted laws and policies which over-ride the decisions made by tenants, landlords, builders, home buyers, and others involved in the private marketplace. One of the most common of these interventions have been "slum-clearance" programs. Other interventions include laws intended to either promote or prevent the racial segregation of housing, as well as the direct building of public housing.

Slum Clearance

Whether called "slum clearance" in the nineteenth century or "urban renewal" in the twentieth century, government programs to demolish housing considered unsatisfactory by third party observers have displaced vast numbers of low-income tenants, often supposedly for their own good. However, all this activity, expense, and disruptions of lives, is based on the crucial—and unsubstantiated—assumption that third parties who pay no costs know better what is good for low-income tenants than those tenants themselves do.

Slum clearance programs in the nineteenth century created no new housing and urban renewal programs in the twentieth century created fewer low-income housing units than they destroyed, with rents on many of these new units being beyond the price range that the displaced tenants could afford. The net result was that these programs restricted, rather than expanded, the options available to low-income tenants. However disagreeable the pre-existing housing may have looked to journalists or social reformers, the tenants who lived there would obviously have been living in better housing if they could have afforded it—consistent with their other goals and desires.

Even famed nineteenth-century crusading journalist Jacob Riis noted in passing that Jewish immigrants packed into crowded slums on New York's lower east side saved a substantial proportion of their incomes. Clearly they had other goals besides maximizing the space, comfort, or amenities of the housing in which they lived. When slum clearance forced them to move into housing more pleasing to third-party observers, the costs of this upgrading had to be paid by the tenants, not the observers, and it would come at the expense of the tenants' other goals and desires. Among these other uses of their incomes was sending money to family members in Europe who were often suffering both economic deprivation and social persecution, including mob violence.

Most of the Jewish immigrants to America came with their passage across the Atlantic paid by family members already living in the United States. In an earlier generation, the same was true of the Irish, who likewise lived in slums and yet came up with the money to pay to rescue their families in Ireland from the great famine there in the 1840s and to bring millions of them to America.

There is no question that early Jewish immigrants lived in over-crowded tenements under conditions that most other Americans considered appalling. When the lower east side of New York was a predominantly Jewish slum, it contained three times as many people per square mile as it did when it was a low-income ghetto for other groups a hundred years later. Half of the Jews in this nineteenth century ghetto slept three or four to a room, and nearly one-fourth slept five to a room. Moreover, mid-nineteenth century slums had toilets in the yards and alleys behind the building. Only later in that century did running water come into the buildings themselves, to be *shared* by the tenants, who jointly had access to the same water faucets and toilets. In 1894, there were only 51 private toilets in nearly 4,000 tenements and only 306 persons out of more than a quarter of a million had bathtubs in their homes.

There was no question that the housing in which these people lived left a lot to be desired. But there were other things that they also desired—such as saving their families abroad from starvation and from death at the hands of anti-semitic mobs. Moreover, they were also thinking beyond their immediate circumstances to a better future for themselves and their children in America. Their savings helped prepare for that future, which turned out to be far better than most people might have imagined at the time. What slum clearance did was force these and other slum tenants to use some of their hard-earned incomes to finance housing that left third-party observers feeling better, though these tenants could have moved into such more expensive housing before if they had considered it worth the other things they would have to sacrifice to do so.

During the same era, Italian immigrants—mostly men—lived in housing that was at least as appalling in New York and in other cities in Europe and South America. Yet, by enduring miserable living conditions, and often skimping on their own food, these men were able to save, enabling them to send money back to Italy to maintain their families there until their savings reached the point where they could either return to Italy to make a better life there or else bring their families over to join them in America. In both cases, they and their families rose economically over the years. But that rise was not helped when social reformers, armed with the power of government, forced them to buy more or better housing than they wanted at the time. In a later era, it was different minority groups who were displaced by urban renewal. A landmark study of urban renewal programs in the 1950s found that more than three-fifths of the people displaced were either blacks or Puerto Ricans.

It is always possible to make people better off in one dimension, such as housing, at the cost of making them worse off in other dimensions that are not so visible to third-party observers. Where this must be done against their will, by imposing the power of government through slum-clearance programs, it is by no means clear that the supposed beneficiaries of these programs are better off on net balance. Would the slums never have been cleared otherwise? One way to test this would be to consider another nineteenth-century poverty-stricken group living in substandard housing whom housing reformers overlooked at the time—the newly freed blacks in the South.

When the Civil War ended, blacks were still living in the same log cabins with dirt floors that they had lived in as slaves. Such amenities as window panes were nearly unknown among the former slaves at this point. Yet, without anyone crusading for better housing for blacks, the ordinary pressures of the marketplace led to improvements in the housing that blacks lived in. This happened not only where blacks owned or rented their homes but also where they lived in housing supplied by white landowners for whom they worked as laborers or as sharecroppers. Competition for labor forced whites who were supplying the housing for some of the blacks who worked for them, and enabled other blacks whose incomes were gradually rising over the years, to slowly but surely improve the housing that black families lived in. Log cabins were replaced by frame houses, dirt floors were covered by planks and, by the turn of the century, glass window panes began to appear. The kind of housing which blacks had inhabited at the end of the Civil War had almost totally disappeared by the turn of the century—without any slum clearance or other housing crusades.

The houses that blacks lived in at this juncture were still lacking many amenities that would come later but both the previous and the future improvements would come without the intervention of social reformers and the government, unlike what was happening in Northern immigrant slums. As of 1896, urban blacks—still mostly living in the South—had an average of three rooms per family. This was crowded in that era of large families, though less crowded than among the Jews or Italians in New York at that same time. The bottom line is that bad housing improved over time as people's productive capacity, and consequently their incomes, rose—with or without social reformers and slum clearance programs. The only people who unequivocally benefitted from these programs were those who ran them and social reformers who promoted them, making themselves feel both good and important.

Racial Segregation

The residential clustering or segregation of particular groups has been the rule, rather than the exception, in countries around the world and over the centuries. While this has been strikingly visible to the naked eye when the groups were different in appearance, as with blacks and whites in the United States, the same phenomenon has been common where the differences could not be seen with the naked eye.

Sometimes the groups cluster spontaneously and sometimes they are found clustered because they have been rejected by other groups, who don't want them living in their neighborhoods, and sometimes governing authorities assign them to separate living areas. The term "ghetto" originated centuries ago in Europe, to describe the neighborhoods where Jews were confined, sometimes behind walls that were closed off at night. But Ibos from southern Nigeria were likewise confined to separate neighborhoods in northern Nigeria, even though both groups were black Africans whom others might have had difficulty telling apart. In earlier centuries, the Chinese minorities in Southeast Asia were often likewise confined to neighborhoods prescribed by the ruling authorities, rather than being allowed to live at random among the indigenous populations or among their European overlords.

In late-twentieth century Brazil, where racial distinctions were broken down into "browns," "blacks" and "whites," the browns and blacks were more residentially separate from one another than the browns were from the whites. However, this was not a result of orders from political authorities. In late-twentieth century America, it was found that "51.65 per cent of the population of Southern European origin would have to be redistributed in order to achieve full integration with the Northern European population."

The term "segregation" has often been used to describe both spontaneous residential group clustering and residential separation imposed by authorities. In its strict sense, the term is used to refer to the latter. An intermediate pattern is group clustering due to an inability of a particular group to find acceptance—or perhaps even toleration—in communities of other groups. There are also combinations. For example, for most of the twentieth century, blacks in Manhattan were largely confined to Harlem because they were not welcome in other neighborhoods. However, within Harlem, there were further clusterings of people voluntarily, according to their incomes, education, and times of arrival from the South, the more fortunate blacks living on the outer regions of Harlem and leading the expansion of the community into surrounding white neighborhoods. It was much the same story on New York's lower east side during the immigrant era, when Polish, Hungarian, and Romanian Jews lived clustered separately within the larger Jewish enclave.

Many lament racial or ethnic residential clustering and see it as a "problem" to be "solved." However, affinities of culture, kinship, and language have led many people to prefer to live among their own groups, even when opportunities were available to live elsewhere. The immigrant generation, still speaking a foreign language, tended to cling to neighborhoods where they could communicate with others from the same country, even after they had moved up economically and could afford to move on to more prosperous neighborhoods inhabited by the native born or indigenous population. Second and later generations, who tended to be more acculturated, could more readily move out of ethnic enclaves and into the mainstream of the larger society—which was correspondingly less resistant to their moving into the new neighborhoods.

In other words, there may not be a fixed amount of "racism" or other aversions restricting the residential housing of a given group. Changes within the group itself over time can change the degree of acceptance or resistance, as the costs of associating with them change. Perhaps the most telling example of these changes involves the history of the black population of the United States, especially in urban areas. Long before slavery ended, there were individual blacks who became free in one way or another and there were about half a million of them in the middle of the nineteenth century. As they changed, their housing options changed. Many of the blacks living in Northern cities were escaped slaves or their children, lacking in acculturation to the world in which they were now living. As of the middle of the nineteenth century, these free blacks in the North as well as the South were socially unaccepted, not only as regards housing but also in terms of being denied access to public accommodations open to others. With the passing years and generations, however, these blacks became more acculturated—and faced declining resistance to their participation in the life of the larger community.

By contemporary accounts, the Northern black communities were becoming cleaner, safer, and more self-supporting in the nineteenth century. Jacob Riis reported at the time "a distinct and gratifying improvement" among blacks in New York City and a modern historian has noted that blacks in New York were better off at this point than most recent white immigrants, with black waiters receiving higher pay than Irish waiters and black construction worker employed building the Croton reservoir receiving higher pay than Italian workers on the same project. W. E. B. DuBois reported similar progress in nineteenth-century Philadelphia, where black cooks and waiters had graduated into the ranks of some of the leading caterers in the city, winning "respect for their people" in the process.

DuBois also noted in 1899 "a growing liberal spirit toward the Negro in Philadelphia," in which "the community was disposed to throw off the trammels, brush away petty hindrances and to soften the harshness of race prejudice," including "a greater freedom of domicile" in more recent times. There were parallel developments in Chicago, Detroit and other Northern communities, so that "an unprecedented period of racial amity and integration" developed in the period from 1870 to 1890, and there was much optimism that race relations would continue to improve, in the North at least, in the twentieth century. In reality, however, this era was followed by an era of dramatic retrogressions in race relations in the North. These were not just inexplicable swings of the pendulum in white public opinion. In both the era of progress and the era of retrogression, realities changed and opinions changed in their wake.

Just as the unacculturated blacks who first settled in the North in the pre-Civil War era had met with negative reactions from the white population, so too did the vastly larger numbers of largely unacculturated blacks who formed the great migration out of the South that began at the end of the nineteenth century and continued for decades into the twentieth century. The most striking example of this retrogression was the development of black ghettoes that continued to exist on into the twenty-first century. Such ghettoes had not yet begun to develop in most Northern cities at the end of the nineteenth century. It was not just that these cities did not yet have the massive black populations that they would have after the great migrations from the South. Whatever black populations they did have tended to live dispersed among the white population.

As late as 1910, more than two-thirds of the black population in Chicago lived in neighborhoods that were predominantly white and as early as 1860, while most blacks in Detroit tended to live clustered in a particular area, even within that area there was no street where even half of the inhabitants were black. Similarly in New York, Philadelphia, and Washington, there was some clustering of blacks, as other groups clustered, but there were no all-black neighborhoods, such as would become common later on. It was not simply that the mass migrations out of the South produced larger clusters of blacks in Northern cities. Blacks now began to be *excluded* from white neighborhoods in which they had been able to live before. In 1911, Baltimore passed its first housing segregation law. The Ku Klux Klan began to expand into the North.

"Racism" cannot be cited as an explanation of these trends, as if it were some independent cause, rather than a characterization of changing attitudes which themselves require explanation. It was not only whites, but also existing members of Northern black communities, who resented the new arrivals from the South. The black press denounced these migrants from the South as crude, vulgar, unwashed, rowdy, and criminal—and as a menace to the standing of the whole race in the eyes of the larger white community. As the Southern migrants became the vast majority of the black population in Northern cities, barriers went up against all blacks in housing, as well as in employment.

None of this was unique to blacks. In an earlier era, the Irish were unwelcome as neighbors—and this too was not merely a matter of "perceptions," "stereotypes," or other wholly subjective factors. Cholera was unknown in American cities before the massive influx of Irish immigrants, beginning in the 1840s, when a cholera epidemic struck Boston, almost exclusively in Irish neighborhoods. The same disease struck disproportionately in Irish neighborhoods in New York. Tuberculosis and alcoholism also plagued Irish communities in various cities. Irish neighborhoods were also tough neighborhoods. In New York, the predominantly Irish Sixth Ward was known as "the bloody ould Sixth" another as "Hell's Kitchen," and still another as "San Juan Hill" because the battles there were reminiscent of the battle of San Juan Hill in the Spanish-American war. Irish neighborhoods in other cities had similar names for similar reasons.

The resistance to the Irish moving into other neighborhoods was not simply a matter of inexplicable "perceptions" or "stereotypes." However, as the Irish themselves changed over the generations, attitudes toward them also changed, as reflected in their greater acceptance in housing, as well as in employment, where the stock phrase, "No Irish Need Apply" faded away over time. All housing segregation has not been spontaneous. As already noted, Baltimore passed a housing segregation law in 1911. It was one of a number of municipal governments to make racial segregation in housing a policy in the twentieth century. The federal government likewise promoted segregation. The Federal Housing Administration refused to make government-insured housing loans unless the housing was racially segregated, on into the late 1940s. The fact that the government later reversed this policy and began to place blacks in neighborhoods that were previously all white does not mean that government is necessarily for or against racial segregation. It all depends on the attitudes and the politics of the times. Moreover, the economics of housing segregation differs from the politics of it.

Where black ghettoes expand into previously all-white neighborhoods through the operations of the marketplace, such expansion has tended to be led by better-educated and higher-income individuals already living on the periphery of the ghetto. These are the kinds of people likely to encounter less resistance than lower-income, more poorly educated, and more violent people farther inside the ghetto. But, where racial integration is promoted by government, those blacks inserted into white communities via housing projects or individually subsidized housing tend to be those with lower incomes, poorer education, and higher crime rates.

Either kind of ghetto expansion can and has encountered resistance. But the resistance to the government programs has tended to be much more vehement. Nor can this resistance all be attributed to racism. Indeed, some black middle-class communities have bitterly resisted the transplanting into their midst of the kind of people they have sought to escape by moving out of the ghetto.

IMPLICATIONS

The economics of housing is very different from the politics of housing. In the politics of housing, issues can be framed in terms of the desirability of various goals, such as "affordable housing" or "open space." The economics of housing can only make us aware of the costs of our goals—and that these costs are inescapable, whether or not we acknowledge their existence or assess their magnitude.

Politics offers attractive solutions but economics can offer only trade-offs. For example, when laws are proposed to restrict the height of apartment buildings in a community, politics presents the issue in terms of whether we prefer tall buildings or buildings of more modest height in our town. Economics asks what you are prepared to trade off in order to keep the height of buildings below some specified level. In places where land costs may equal or exceed the cost of the apartment buildings themselves, the difference between allowing ten-story buildings to be built and allowing a maximum of five stories may be that rents will be twice as high in the shorter buildings. The question then is not simply whether you prefer shorter buildings but *how much* do you prefer shorter buildings and what price are you prepared to pay to mandate height restrictions in your community. A doubling of rents and three additional highway fatalities per year? A tripling of rents and six additional highway fatalities per year?

Economics cannot answer such questions. It can only make you aware of a need to ask them. Economics was christened "the dismal science" because it dealt with inescapable constraints and painful trade-offs, instead of the more pleasant and unbounded visions, and their accompanying rhetoric, which many find so attractive. Moreover, economics follows the unfolding consequences of decisions over time, not just what happens in stage one, which may indeed seem to fulfill the hopes that inspired these decisions. Nowhere are the consequences more long-lasting than in housing, where a community can have an aging and shrinking supply of apartment buildings, with accompanying housing shortages, for decades, or even generations, after the rent control laws which lead to such consequences.

The passage of time insulates many political decisions from public awareness of their real consequences. Only a small fraction of New Yorkers today are old enough to remember what the housing situation was there before rent control laws were introduced during World War II. Only a dwindling number of Californians are old enough to remember when that state's housing prices were very much like housing prices in the rest of the country, instead of being some multiple of what people pay elsewhere for a home or an apartment. These and other consequences of particular political decisions in the past are today just "facts of life" that new generations have grown up with as something as natural as the weather or other circumstances of their existence.

The vast numbers of frustrated California motorists who endure long commutes to and from work on congested highways are unlikely to see any connection between their daily frustrations and attractive-sounding policies about "open space" or "farmland preservation." Nor are economists who point out that connection likely to be as popular with them as politicians who are ready to offer solutions to rescue these motorists from their current problems, using the same kind of one-stage thinking that created these problems in the first place.

Chapter 5

Risky Business

> The American Statistical Association offered at their annual meeting a T-shirt bearing the motto: "Uncertainty: One Thing You Can Always Count on."

Nothing is more certain than risk. The insurance business is just one of the ways of dealing with risk. Having government agencies come to the aid of disaster victims is another. Mutual aid societies helped victims of social or natural disasters long before there were government agencies charged with this task. Individuals have spread their own risks in various ways and families have sought to safeguard their members for centuries—longer than any other institution has taken on the task of cushioning people against the inescapable risks of life.

Whatever social mechanisms are used to deal with risk seek to do two crucial things: (1) reduce the magnitude of risk and (2) transfer that risk to whoever can bear it at the lowest cost. Where the transfer of risk is accompanied by a reduction of risk this process makes it mutually beneficial for the person initially at risk to pay someone else to share the risk or to carry the risk completely. This in turn means that society as a whole benefits from having its risks minimized and the resources put aside for dealing with them reduced, making those resources available for other uses.

Merely providing information or assessments of risk is also a valuable service, for which credit-rating services are paid, whether these are companies like TRW that provide businesses with information on the credit history of individual consumers, or companies like Moody's or Standard & Poor's which rate the relative risks of bonds issued by businesses themselves, states, or nations, so that investors can be guided accordingly.

When trade associations of insurance companies test automobiles for safety in crash tests, that likewise creates benefits for the companies in these associations, by allowing them to determine how much to charge to insure different vehicles, and it also assists consumers in making choices of which kinds, makes, and models of vehicles to buy. Consumer choices in turn influence automobile manufacturers as to what kinds of safety provisions to add to their cars, in order to compete successfully, leading cars in general to become safer over time.

To some extent, reducing risk through insurance may cause people to take more risks. Just as lower prices for other things usually cause more to be demanded, so lowering the costs of given risks enables people to take on additional risks. Distinguished economist Joseph Schumpeter pointed out that cars travel faster because they have brakes.

If you were driving a car without brakes, or with brakes that you knew to be completely ineffective, it would be foolhardy to drive faster than 10 or 15 miles per hour. At a sufficiently slow speed on a sufficiently uncrowded road, you might be able to depend on simply taking your foot off the gas and letting the car coast to a stop. But, when you have well-functioning brakes as a risk-reducing device, you may well drive 60 miles an hour on a crowded highway. Thus brakes reduce the dangers in a given situation but also encourage people to drive in more dangerous situations than they would otherwise. This does not mean that safety devices are futile. It means that the benefits of such devices include benefits over and beyond any benefits from net reductions of risk. For example, because cars are able to travel at higher speeds, more extensive travel for business or pleasure becomes feasible.

Similarly, when you have automobile insurance, you may drive over to visit an old friend or family member who lives in a high crime neighborhood, where you might not risk parking your car if it were not insured, for fear of theft or vandalism. While you would still not want to have your car stolen or damaged, the chance of that happening may become an affordable risk when car insurance covers that possibility. Whether on net balance one lives a less risky life as a result of insurance is not always certain. But, even if there is no net reduction in risk, there may be other benefits resulting from the insurance. In addition to visiting places where the risk would be too great otherwise, one may live up in the hills in a home with a spectacular view, even if that home is somewhat more at risk of fire because it is surrounded by trees and is on a narrow winding road that would impede a fire truck from reaching the home in an emergency as quickly as it could down in the flatlands.

In addition to insurance companies which charge for the service of carrying other people's risks, there are businesses which incorporate charges for risk in the prices they charge for other goods and services. Indeed, all businesses must include some charge for risk in their prices, though this is usually noticeable only in businesses which charge more than usual for the same goods that are available more cheaply elsewhere because local risks are higher than in other neighborhoods. Moreover, some risks are in effect paid for not in money, but by a reduction in the number of businesses willing to locate in less desirable neighborhoods, or in countries where debts are hard to collect or where crime, vandalism, and terrorist activity reduce personal safety.

In some low-income neighborhoods with a history of riots, vandalism, and shoplifting, the local inhabitants—most of whom may well be honest and decent people—pay the costs created by those among them who are not by having lower quantities and qualities of goods and services available to them locally, and at higher prices. Many of these local inhabitants may be forced to go elsewhere for shopping or to get their paychecks cashed. For example, a study in Oakland, California, found:

> Less than half (46 percent) of Oakland's low-income consumers surveyed said that they did their banking in their neighborhoods. However, 71 percent of middle-income area respondents said that they did their banking in their own neighborhoods.

The same study found that it was six times as common among Oakland's low-income residents as among its middle-income residents to use checking-cashing centers instead of banks. With shopping as well, low-income consumers have often found themselves forced to go elsewhere to get things that were either unavailable nearby or not available in as good a quality or as low a price as in higher-income neighborhoods. For example, this survey found low-income consumers spending only about a third of their money shopping in their local community and two-thirds shopping elsewhere.

While all this is easy to understand from an economic perspective, it is also easy to distort from a political perspective. Blaming the owners of local stores and check-cashing agencies for the higher charges in such places, compared to charges in safer middle-class neighborhoods, is usually more politically effective than blaming those local inhabitants who create the costs which these institutions pass along to customers—especially if the business owners are mostly of a different ethnic background than the local people. Even without the incentives of politics, many observers who do not think beyond stage one blame high prices on those who charge these prices, rather than on those who create the additional risks and costs which these prices reflect. From this it is a short step to advocating laws and policies to restrict how high local prices or local check-cashing charges or interest rates will be allowed to go.

However plausible such laws and policies might seem to those who do not think beyond stage one, the net result of preventing local businesses from recovering the higher local costs in the prices they charge is likely to be a reduction in the number of businesses that can earn as much locally as elsewhere—or that can even earn enough to survive locally. Given the existing meager availability of businesses in many low-income neighborhoods, anything that forces more local businesses to close aggravates the problems of the people living there.

Banco Popular, which operates a check-cashing service in low-income Hispanic neighborhoods, has charged 1.1 percent of the value of the checks it cashes, plus 20 cents a check. This means that someone earning $300 a week pays $3.50 per week to get a paycheck cashed. Meanwhile, someone earning ten times as much money probably pays nothing, since banks are happy to have high-income people among their customers and make money off the large savings accounts and checking accounts which such people typically have, while the dangers of default are less. For the low-income worker, the question is whether taking a bus or taxi to try to get a paycheck cashed will cost more than the $3.50 paid to Banco Popular, which has armored cars that drive up to the employer's place of business on pay day.

While Banco Popular's check-cashing service charges for what many banks provide free, it also takes bigger risks of losses. The workers who cash their paychecks may be honest and the checks genuine, but some of the employers they work for are small fly-by-night operators, who may suddenly leave town, closing their bank accounts and taking their money with them, making their workers' paychecks worthless. Just one such dishonest employer cost Banco Popular $66,000 in cashed paychecks that could not be redeemed at the bank where the employer's account had been closed before he skipped town. That is far less likely to happen with a paycheck from someone who earns $3,000 a week than with someone who earns $300 a week. Little fly-by-night operators are unlikely to be paying their employees $156,000 a year. People with such high incomes are more likely to be working for more substantial and reliable businesses and organizations.

The risks and costs of cashing checks for low-income people, or lending money to them, are inherent in the circumstances, rather than in the particular institutions which handle these risks. When a reputable bank that normally serves middle class or affluent people opens an affiliate in low-income neighborhoods, it faces those same risks—but without as much experience in dealing with them. Operating in what is called the "subprime market"—where borrowers do not have as good credit ratings as in the prime markets—these banks, as the *Wall Street Journal* put it, began "to realize that the market was far tougher than they had expected." Even charging interest rates ranging from 12 percent to 24 percent in making riskier loans to low-income borrowers—compared to 7 or 8 percent on other loans—the higher rates of default often made these loans unprofitable.

Bank of America, for example, lost hundreds of millions of dollars on such loans. In 2001, according to the *Wall Street Journal*, Bank of America "said its 96 EquiCredit Corp. offices across the US. will stop making subprime loans immediately." Other banks were apparently not quick enough in closing down such losing operations. A large Chicago bank went out of business, with losses on subprime loans being singled out as the main reason. Losses on such loans were also cited by the Federal Deposit Insurance Corporation as a factor in the closing of 7 out of 19 banks that failed. The Federal Housing Authority, which usually lends to lower-income home buyers, has had a repayment delinquency rate more than triple that of those who lend to other home buyers.

RISK-REDUCING INSTITUTIONS

Families, gangs, feudal warlords, insurance companies, partnerships, commodity speculators, and issuers of stocks and bonds are all in the business of reducing and transferring risk.

All face the problem that reducing existing riskiness increases the willingness of the protected individual to take more risks. An individual who belongs to a tough gang may become more belligerent towards other individuals he encounters than he would be without the protection afforded by the gang's reputation. In medieval times, a peasant might be reluctant to farm in some areas where there were robbers and marauders around, without the protection of the armed nobility who take part of the peasant's produce as payment for their services. Though called tribute, these payments—usually in kind—amounted to insurance premiums.

Those who are in the business of selling insurance try to take into account not only the existing risks, but also the increased amount of risky behavior that the policy holder may engage in as a result of becoming insured. For similar reasons, the family—the oldest insurer of all—cautions its members, both when they are growing up and on specific occasions afterwards, against various kinds of risky behavior. When families had the burden of taking care of an unwed daughter's baby, there was more chaperoning, screening of her associates, and moral stigma attached to unwed motherhood. All these things declined or disappeared after many of these costs were shifted to government agencies.

Government Agencies

The incentives of a government agency are very different from those of a family or an insurance company. As a matter of financial self-protection, both families and insurance companies must seek to discourage risky behavior in one way or another. For a government agency, however, financed by taxpayers' money, there is no such urgency about discouraging the increased risks that people may take because those risks are covered by others. Moreover, the agency gets its biggest political support from helping, not criticizing. Thus government emergency programs to help people struck by floods, hurricanes, and other natural disasters make it easier for people whose homes have been destroyed to rebuild at the same locations, in areas where such disasters recur regularly over the years. Similarly, government programs to develop medicines and medical procedures to deal with AIDS, at costs subsidized by the taxpayers, have led to a resurgence of the kinds of risky behaviors that can lead to AIDS.

Similar incentives produce similar results at the international level. Where both national and international institutions stand ready to bail out governments facing bankruptcy and likely to have defaults on its debts that would hurt banks and other investors in other countries, the prospects of such bailouts allows private financial institutions to invest in countries where it would be too risky to invest otherwise. Sporadic calls for a "restructuring" of debt[1] or a "forgiveness" of Third World debt encourage the debtor governments to borrow more money than they would if they knew that

---

[1]Essentially paying off old debts with new loans.

the loans would have to be repaid or an open declaration of bank-ruptcy announced, which would make it harder to borrow again, perhaps for many years. International financial crises, especially those involving poorer countries, often bring out one-stage think-ing among those who wish to help less fortunate people, with the longer run consequences being overlooked.

Since risk is inescapable, the question of how much risk to toler-ate is a question of weighing one cost against another. Often this is not done, especially when those who make such decisions do not pay the costs of these decisions and do not think beyond stage one. For example, when a certain number of children receive in-juries from playing in a particular playground, then the swings, seesaws, or other equipment in that playground may be blamed and perhaps removed, or those responsible for the playground may be sued. But, if the offending equipment is removed or the play-ground shut down because of lawsuits or the fear of lawsuits, will the children be safer?

Suppose that X percent of the children will receive serious injuries if they play in this particular playground and 2X percent will receive equally serious injuries if they stay home. Since no place is 100 per-cent safe, and none can be made 100 percent safe, the only mean-ingful question is the relative safety of one place compared to another and the cost of making either place safer by a given amount. Our natural inclination may be to want to make every place as safe as possible but in reality no one does that when they must pay the costs themselves. We are willing to pay for brakes in our cars, but having a second set of brakes in case the first set fails would make us safer still, and a third set would result in still more reduction of risk, though probably not by a substantial amount. However, faced with rising costs and declining reductions of risk as backup brakes are added to automobiles, most people will at some point refuse to pay any more for additional insignificant reductions in risk.

However, if someone else is paying for reductions in risk, the point at which risk reduction stops may be very different. Lawsuits may impose costs that shut down a playground which is safer than any alternative place the children are likely to be, including their homes. In short, when someone else is paying, small risks may be paid for at costs that include incurring larger risks for other people in the future. The implicit assumption that zero risk can be taken as a benchmark for assessing blame for particular risks can easily lead to higher risks than if it was understood from the outset that one risk must be weighed against another, not compared to zero risk or even to some arbitrary standard of "acceptable" versus "unacceptable" risk.

Ownership Sharing

Sharing ownership has long been another way of reducing risks. Back in the days of wooden sailing ships, the danger that one of these ships would be lost at sea was much greater than today. Some shipowners protected themselves by not owning a given ship alone, but instead owning for example one-tenth of a share in ten different ships. While the increased number of ships meant a greater risk that one of these vessels would sink, it also reduced the likelihood that the loss would be as catastrophic as if one owned a single ship outright. Obviously, those shipowners who were rich enough to own a whole fleet of ships outright could spread the risk that way.

Modern corporations similarly make it possible for individuals to spread their risks by owning stock in a number of different businesses, without owning any particular business outright. However, employees who own stock in the businesses they work for do not get the full benefits of risk spreading, since both their jobs and the money they will depend on when they no longer have jobs—

whether due to unemployment or retirement—depend on the fate of the same company. The consequences of concentrating risks, instead of spreading them, proved to be catastrophic for many employees of corporations that went bankrupt amid various well-publicized scandals among American corporations in 2002.

Not only businesses, but workmen as well, have long pooled their risks as a way of making them less onerous to individuals. Mutual aid societies have arisen among workers in a given occupation or industry, or members of a particular ethnic group, or residents in a given neighborhood. By paying small amounts into a common fund, members of mutual aid societies enabled those among them who were stricken by illness or disabled by injuries to have the financial consequences cushioned by payments from the fund. Here the dangers of deliberately engaging in more risky behavior were minimized, first of all by the prospect of pain and death, but also by the fact of being known by other members of the mutual aid society, who could monitor malingering or fraudulent claims better than larger and more impersonal institutions could.

Safety Movements

A very different kind of institution for dealing with risk has arisen in more recent times. This is the private organization or movement devoted to imposing safety requirements through publicity, litigation or regulation. These include "public interest" law firms, ideological organizations and movements, such as the so-called Center for Science in the Public Interest, and government agencies such as the National Highway Safety Administration. Since these organizations do not charge directly for their services like mutual aid societies or insurance companies, they must collect the money needed to support themselves from lawsuits, donations, or taxes. Put differently, their only money-making product or service is fear—and their incentives are to induce as much fear as possible in jurors, legislators, and the general public.

Whereas individuals weighing risks for themselves are restrained in how much risk reduction they will seek by the costs, there are no such restraints on the amount of risk reduction sought by those whose risk reduction is paid for with other people's money. Nor is there any such inherent restraint on how much fear they will generate from a given risk or how much credit they will claim for whatever risk reduction may take place, regardless of what the facts may be.

Automobile safety is a classic example of third party safety decisions by organizations and movements whose money and power come from producing fear. Third-party safety crusades operate in some ways the opposite from risk-reduction processes in which those who are at risk choose alternatives for themselves and pay the costs themselves. The central question of how much risk is to be reduced at what costs is usually not raised at all by third-party safety organizations or movements. Nor are alternative risks weighed against one another. Instead, the theme is that something is "unsafe" and therefore needs to be made safe. The argument is essentially that existing risks show that current safeguards are inadequate and/or the people in control of them are insufficiently conscientious, or both. Therefore power and money need to be vested in new people and new institutions, in order to protect the public—according to this argument.

This kind of argument can be applied to almost anything, since nothing is literally 100 percent safe. It has been used against medications, pesticides, nuclear power, automobiles, and many other targets. Where the issue is the safety of nuclear power plants, for example, the answer to the question whether nuclear power is safe is obviously *No!* If nuclear power were safe, it would be the only safe thing on the face of the earth. This page that you are reading isn't safe. It can catch fire, which can spread and burn down your home, with you in it. The only meaningful question, to those who are spending their own money to deal with their own risks, is whether it is worth what it would cost to fireproof every page in every book, magazine, or newspaper.

In the case of nuclear power, the question of safety, in addition to cost, is *Compared to what?* Compared to generating electricity with hydroelectric dams or the burning of fossil fuels or compared to reducing our use of electricity with dimmer lights or foregoing the use of many things that are run by electricity and taking our chances on alternative power sources? Once the discussion changes to a discussion of incremental trade-offs, then nuclear power becomes one of the safest options. But neither it nor anything else is categorically safe.

These kinds of questions, which are central to safety decisions made by those who pay the costs, are conspicuous by their absence in third-party safety crusades. The rise of third-party safety advocates in the latter part of the twentieth century has brought with it categorical rhetoric in place of incremental analysis, and incentives to maximize fears rather than to minimize net injuries and deaths. A landmark in these trends was the 1965 book *Unsafe at Any Speed* by Ralph Nader, attacking the safety of American automobiles in general and a car called the Corvair in particular. This book was not only historically important, as the beginning of a major political trend, but was also important in setting a pattern in methods of persuasion that have been followed by many other publications, politicians, and organizations in dealing with issues of risk and safety. This pattern is therefore worth scrutinizing, even many decades later.

The thesis of *Unsafe at Any Speed* was that American cars were unsafe because safety was neglected by automobile manufacturers, in order to save on manufacturing costs and not interfere with styling, as some safety devices might. Consumers were depicted as helpless to do anything about safety and therefore as needing government intervention for their protection.

According to Nader, "users of vehicles" are "in no position to dictate safer automobile design." Put differently: "The American automobile is produced exclusively to the standards which the manufacturer decides to establish." More generally, one of the "great problems of contemporary life is how to control the power of economic interests which ignore the harmful effects of their applied science and technology."

Unsafe at Any Speed was a masterpiece in the art of persuasion, successfully establishing several crucial beliefs about the automobile industry in general, and about the Corvair in particular, without hard evidence being either offered or asked for. The first of these beliefs is that American automobiles are dangerous and becoming more so. As Nader put it, in the first sentence of his preface:

> For over half a century the automobile has brought death, injury, and the most inestimable sorrow and deprivation to millions of people. With Medea-like intensity, this mass trauma began rising sharply four years ago reflecting new and unexpected ravages by the motor vehicle.

Anecdotes and selective quotations abounded to *insinuate* the conclusions reached, but nowhere did Nader present automobile accident fatality rates in America over time, for the United States versus other countries, for the Corvair versus other automobiles, or for countries where automobiles are produced under capitalist incentives versus countries where the industry is under socialist management. Such data would have supported none of the conclusions reached. The masterpiece was in making such empirical support unnecessary through various rhetorical devices. For example, he quoted a critic who characterized the Corvair as "probably the worst riding, worst all-around handling car available to the American public." and Nader attributed this to "engineering and management operations within General Motors which led to such an unsafe vehicle." Experts who assessed the Corvair and its handling more favorably—some enthusiastically—were of course not quoted.

Despite Nader's sweeping assertions about what had been happening over a period of "half a century," he offered no statistical data covering that span and the data that were available showed long-term trends that were the direct opposite of what *Unsafe at Any Speed* implied. While it was true, as Nader claimed, that automobile accidents were rising, it was also true that the population of the country was rising, the numbers of cars on the road were rising, and the miles they were traveling were rising. In proportion to population, automobile fatality rates when *Unsafe at Any Speed* was published in 1965 were less than half of what they had been back in the 1920s. In proportion to millions of vehicle-miles driven, the fatality rate was less than one-third of what it had been in the 1920s.

There are fluctuations in these rates, as with most statistics over long periods of time, and in the years immediately before publication of *Unsafe at Any Speed* there had been a slight upward trend. But during all the previous decades of presumably helpless consumers, corporate greed, and inadequate government regulation, the safety of American automobiles had been improving dramatically, as shown by fatality rates a fraction of what they had once been, despite more crowded roadways and higher speeds. Yet the continuation of this decades-long trend toward reduced automobile fatality rates was later credited by safety advocates and much of the media to the creation of a federal agency to regulate automobile safety, in response to Ralph Nader's book. This conclusion was reached by the simple expedient of ignoring the previous history and counting the "lives saved" as the long trend of declining fatality rates continued.

What of the Corvair? Here Nader scored his greatest success. The bad publicity he unleashed was reflected in falling sales that forced General Motors to discontinue production of the car. Years later, extensive tests by the U. S. Department of Transportation showed that the Corvair's safety was comparable to that of similar cars of its era, and concluded that the performance of the Corvair "is at least as good as the performance of some contemporary vehicles both foreign and domestic." By then, of course, this information was much too late to matter. The car was extinct—killed off by a safety crusade that set the pattern for later such crusades inspired by Nader's example.

Because of its rear-engine design, the Corvair was indeed more prone to some particular kinds of accidents—and less prone to other kinds of accidents. No matter where an engine is placed, its location affects the physics of the automobile, and therefore the kinds of accidents to which the car is more susceptible and those to which it is less susceptible. Simply by emphasizing the first kinds of accidents—complete with gory examples—and ignoring the second kind, the Corvair could be portrayed as an unsafe car. By similar tactics, almost anything can be made to seem unsafe because ultimately everything is unsafe, if you ignore questions of degree and alternatives.

There are trade-offs not only as regards the placement of an engine, but also as regards the willingness of consumers to pay for all the safety devices that third parties can think of putting on an automobile. However, a trade-off perspective would undermine many, if not most, safety crusades—and not just those about automobiles. Nader dismissed talk of trade-offs as "automobile industry cant"—a rhetorical response making a factual or logical response unnecessary.

Much the same approach has been taken by safety crusaders when it comes to the safety of vaccines and medications, which both save lives and cost lives. No matter how many lives they save, there will still be the inevitable tragedies because some few individuals die as a reaction to being either vaccinated or medicated. (Even a substance as common and generally harmless as peanut butter is literally fatal to some people.) If a particular vaccine is administered to a million children, on most of these children it may have no effect at all—that is, they were not going to catch the disease anyway and they suffer no side effects from the vaccination. But of course no one has any way of knowing in advance which children will be the ones for whom the vaccine will make a difference, one way or another. If 10,000 of those children would have been fatally stricken by the disease from which the vaccine protects them, perhaps 20 will catch that disease from the vaccine itself and die.

Nothing is easier than having a television camera capture the anguish of a mother of one of the 20 dead children, crying and inconsolable in her grief, perhaps blaming herself and wondering aloud whether her child would still be alive if she had not had that child vaccinated. There is no way to know who are the 10,000 other mothers who were spared this anguish because they *did* have their children vaccinated. Nothing is easier for a safety crusader than denouncing the company that produced an "unsafe" vaccine or medicine, without telling the television viewers that there are no other kinds of vaccines or medications—or anything else.

Insurance and Re-insurance

Insurance companies do not simply pay their policy-holders who have suffered various misfortunes. Like families, they seek to reduce the risks that lead to these misfortunes in the first place. While families have more ability to caution and monitor their members than insurance companies have to restrain the risks taken by their policy-holders, insurance companies try to protect themselves financially in other ways. One way is by making the reduction of risk a precondition for issuing an insurance policy or varying the amount charged according to the level of risk. Smokers may be charged higher life insurance premiums than non-smokers. Insurance policies often require the policy-holder to share the costs of risky behavior by paying a fixed amount of the damages incurred—the "deductible"—before the insurance company pays the remainder.

Like a family, an insurance company also reduces its risks by providing individuals with information about those risks. Thus insurance companies often publish booklets on healthy living, safe driving, and ways of avoiding fires and other hazards. Trade associations in the insurance industry test various makes and models of automobiles in crashes and publicize the results, thus informing the public and putting pressure on automobile manufacturers to produce safer cars, in addition to supplying the insurance companies with information on which to base the premiums charged for insuring the different kinds of automobiles. Data on declining automobile fatality rates over time suggest that automobile manufacturers have in fact responded to consumer desires for safety, despite Ralph Nader's rhetoric to the contrary.

Insurance not only reduces risks but transfers those risks to where they can be borne at a lower cost. No one knows when his home might catch fire or his automobile might have an accident but, when an insurance company insures millions of homes and automobiles, its ability to predict in the aggregate is much greater than an individual's ability to predict what will happen individually. Another way of saying the same thing is that the cost of setting aside resources to cover the losses is less for an insurance company than the total of all the resources needed to be set aside by each of the insured individuals to produce the same probability of being able to cover the same costs.

These are not just financial arrangements that benefit particular insurance companies or their policy-holders. From the standpoint of society as a whole, fewer resources are held idle in the economy as a whole when insurance reduces risks and the costs of those risks. Just as owners of homes and businesses transfer their risks of fire, flood, and other damage to insurance companies by paying premiums, so the insurance companies themselves can transfer part of their risks to *re-insurance* companies, at a price. In both cases, risks are not simply transferred but reduced.

If a given insurance company located in the American midwest has a concentration of homeowners' policies in the Ohio valley, a flood in that valley could be financially devastating to that insurance company. However, if it transfers a major part of its liabilities to a re-insurer like the Swiss Reinsurance Company (better known as "Swiss Re"), then this international re-insurer's risk of simultaneous floods in the Ohio valley, the Rhine valley, the Nile valley, the Danube valley, etc., is far less than the local insurance company's risk of a flood in its region.

Since there are well over a hundred re-insurance companies around the world, no single re-insurer may have taken on all the liability for the Ohio Valley, and each re-insurer will have a geographically more widespread set of risks than a local primary insurance company has. In short, the whole insurance and re-insurance industry will have lower risks than any given primary insurance company would have, especially if the primary insurance company has customers concentrated in a particular geographic area. Therefore it is relatively cheaper to insure homes and industries along the banks of various rivers around the world than to insure those along the banks of any one of those rivers.

Put differently, in the absence of re-insurance, enterprises and households in China have to put aside more money, or the physical resources that money represents, to guard against risks than if part of those risks were carried by a company located in Switzerland or the United States, which simultaneously re-insures enterprises and homes in Argentina, Egypt, Australia, Denmark, and Fiji, as well as in China. The amount of equipment and supplies needed to be stockpiled to cope with the risk of floods along the Yangtze River—tents to house people forced from their homes, canned or preserved food to feed them, equipment to repair the damage and rebuild—would be much less if instantaneous electronic transfers of money from Swiss Re could purchase equipment and supplies to be flown in from Japan in a matter of hours, if and when they are needed.

As the London magazine *The Economist* put it, "China is wasting capital that could be used for other things" when it puts aside larger amounts of capital to guard against floods, fires and other catastrophes than it would if it were re-insured by international re-insurers. Insurance, re-insurance and other risk-sharing activities mean that fewer idle resources are necessary around the world to provide a given level of protection against risks. That in turn means that the resources no longer kept idle can be used for other things, such as raising living standards, supporting medical research, or promoting greater economic development.

Lower risks mean lower costs, and market competition among insurance and re-insurance companies means that those lower costs must be passed on to customers in lower premiums, in order to get their business.[2] While geographic distributions of risks pro-

---

[2]For example, *Business Week* magazine reported in its March 4, 2002 issue: "Premiums for reinsurance industrywide had already gone into a tailspin as strong profits attracted more competitors who slashed prices to gain market share." (page 77).

vide one reason for re-insurance, that is not the only reason. For example, more than two-thirds of American life insurance companies also have re-insurance.

As noted in the first chapter, political incentives in response to a natural disaster like the cyclone that struck India in 1999 may be to save face for the Indian government authorities, rather than to rescue the victims as quickly as possible by seeking help from other nations or from international agencies. In a competitive marketplace, however, a private insurance company's reputation for quick response is an enormously valuable asset. It was the Swiss Reinsurance Company's swift response in getting money to the victims of the devastating San Francisco earthquake and fire of 1906 which gained them international renown and promoted the spread of their business around the world.

Although paying off the huge claims resulting from the San Francisco disaster took half the company's annual income from premiums, the subsequent growth in their business as a result led eventually to Swiss Re becoming the world's largest re-insurance company between the two World Wars.

Government Regulation of Insurance

State regulation of insurance companies in the United States adds another dimension to the industry. The politics of insurance regulation can be more complicated than the economics because the very process by which insurance companies reduce risk is often under political attack. For example, some consider it "unfair" that a safe driver with an unblemished record is charged higher insurance premiums because he happens to live in a particular neighborhood where others have more accidents. However, the risks to an automobile do not depend solely on its owner or driver, but also on others who create dangers of accidents, theft, or vandalism.

Similar issues arise when women live longer than men, making it more costly for an insurance company to offer an annuity to a woman than to a man, or when blacks have shorter lifespans than whites, making if more costly to offer life insurance to someone of a given age who is black. Higher automobile accident rates in particular age brackets[3] may also lead to higher premiums for those in these brackets, even when the individual has an unblemished safety record. State laws and regulations may forbid insurance companies from making some or all of these distinctions among people when charging premiums to different policy holders. However, this sense of fairness to individuals can raise risks over all, leading to higher premiums to policy-holders in general.

Two sets of motorists are especially affected by state regulation of automobile insurance rates—very safe drivers and very dangerous drivers. In a free market, the cost of car insurance to the former would be far less than the cost to the latter. However, under political definitions of "fairness," safe drivers can end up subsidizing unsafe drivers, especially when policies are set without thinking beyond stage one.

When the price of auto insurance is set by state officials, often they will not let the price rise to as high a level as it would reach in a free market, when insuring drivers with a record of accidents or serious traffic violations. Since insurance companies will not want to insure such drivers when the premiums they pay are unlikely to cover all the costs caused by these kinds of drivers, a common

---

[3]Although fatality rates from motor vehicle deaths are highest for drivers aged 16 to 19, the declining fatality rates with age end at around age 50 and then rise again, with drivers aged 80 to 84 having nearly as high a fatality rate from motor vehicle deaths as teenagers.

political "solution" is to create a "high-risk" pool of drivers unable to get insurance through regular channels. Insurance companies are then forced to share these high-risk drivers among themselves and rates in general are then set at levels which will enable the insurers to cover the losses created by all their drivers, including those in the high-risk pools.

What this means is that other drivers are subsidizing high-risk drivers. Looking beyond stage one, what this also means is that more pedestrians and motorists are likely to suffer injuries or death because more high-risk drivers can afford to be on the roads and highways than could do so if auto insurance rates were allowed to rise to the very high rates required to compensate for the damage done by reckless drivers. Among the other consequences is that, as rates continue to be held down by government regulators, even in the face of rising costs, a larger and larger percentage of drivers will be unable to obtain insurance through the regular channels and therefore end up in the high-risk pool. In New Jersey, for example, only 12 percent of drivers were in the high-risk pool in the early 1970s but, a decade later, nearly half were.

New Jersey's experience with automobile insurance regulation has not been unique. Nor has automobile insurance been unique in having political criteria over-rule economic criteria in setting insurance rates. The net effect, with other kinds of insurance as well, is to have those with lower risks subsidize those with higher risks, leading to more risky behavior whose consequences can cause both financial losses and losses of life and limb to third parties.

This is not to say that there is never a useful role for government to play when it comes to insurance. Two main problems affect insurance companies in a free market: One problem already discussed earlier is that people who are insured may engage in more risky behavior as a result. This is called "moral hazard." Another is that, when some people choose to be insured for some things and others choose not to be insured, those at the greatest risk are more likely to choose to be insured, so that general statistics on the risks to the population at large are misleading as to the risks of those who choose to buy insurance. That is called "adverse selection."

Government regulation of risky behavior—laws against storing flammable materials in homes or driving under the influence of alcohol, for example—can reduce the risks of moral hazard and laws requiring everyone who drives to have automobile insurance can solve the problem of adverse selection. As in other situations, however, the fact that the government can sometimes improve on the situation that would exist in a free market does not mean that it will in fact restrict its activities to such useful things. When the counterproductive interventions of government in the market are added to its beneficial interventions, it is by no means always clear what the net balance will be.

THE ECONOMICS OF RISK

Safety might seem to be something that you cannot get too much of. Yet everything we do in our everyday lives belies that conclusion. Often what we do makes more sense than what we say. Reducing risks has costs—some of which we are willing to pay and some of which we are not. As already noted, the very paper on which these words are written has risks. So does the water you drink, the food you eat, the oxygen you breathe. Sunshine causes skin cancer. It is not safe to exercise—or not to exercise. The only meaningful question, in all these cases, is the degree of risk, compared to alternatives, and the costs of reducing those risks by given amounts.

Not all costs are money costs. For many people, the cost of reducing risks would be giving up the enjoyment they get from skiing, boating, rock climbing, skateboarding, and other risky activities. In fact, ultimately there are only risky activities, since nothing is 100 percent safe. Yet no one suggests that we retire into passive inactivity—which has its own risks, and which would also have to be away from sunlight if we were consistent, since sunlight increases the risk of skin cancer. On the other hand, most of us are not prepared to walk into a lion's cage or to take a short cut by walking across a freeway during the rush hour. In other words, there are risks we are willing to take and risks we are not willing to take, varying somewhat from person to person, but involving a weighing of benefits and costs in any event. We do not drive to work in tanks, even though tanks would be safer than automobiles, because we are not prepared to pay the costs in either money or commuting time.

However much we may agree with sweeping rhetoric about safety, or even vote for those who use such rhetoric, nevertheless when faced with choices in our own lives we weigh incremental safety against incremental costs. We may consider it worthwhile to avoid one chance in six of getting killed from playing Russian roulette, but not worth it to pay a thousand dollars to avoid one chance in six million of getting killed by some fluke occurrence. Indeed, if the cost of avoiding one chance in six million is merely an inconvenience, some may still refuse to pay it. In short, even those who talk about safety in categorical terms—"if it saves just one life, it is worth whatever it costs"—actually behave in their own lives as if safety is an incremental decision, based on weighing costs against benefits, not a categorical decision.

One of the costs of any given kind of safety may be an increase in other kinds of dangers. It is always possible to make subways safer by having the trains go more slowly, increasing the distances between trains, and having fewer cars per train, in order to reduce the train's weight and hence reduce the distance required to bring the train to a stop. However, all these things reduce the number of passengers who can be carried during rush hours and—since people have to get to work somehow—forces those passengers to try other means of transportation, most of which involve greater risks of death than subway trains do. In short, you can always reduce the risks in subways by policies which increase the risks elsewhere.

During the Second World War, Japanese fighter pilots usually chose not to wear parachutes when going into aerial combat. As one of these pilots explained after the war, although every pilot was provided with a parachute, "the decision to fly without them was our own" and was made because parachutes "hamstring our cockpit movements in a battle," when split-second responses could be matters of life and death, and it "was difficult to move our arms and legs quickly when encumbered by chute straps." In other words, wearing a parachute increased the chances that you would get shot down.[4] Increasing one kind of safety can increase other risks, just as with subway trains and other things.

Here we come to a crucial distinction in decision-making processes—the distinction between individuals making decisions for themselves and third-parties making decisions for others. Subway passengers always have the option of using other means of getting to work, but they are very unlikely to hold subways to a standard of 100 percent safety and go elsewhere if this standard is not met. But what of those who are making decisions for others? If there has recently been a tragic and highly publicized subway accident with a number of fatalities, political outcries for more subway safety may well cause the authorities to order the trains slowed down, fewer cars to be attached to each train, and greater distances maintained between trains.

---

[4]Another reason was that Japanese pilots were usually fighting air battles over enemy territory and bailing out would mean being captured by the enemy, which was "unthinkable" to a Japanese pilot.

Moreover, after the passage of time shows that these policies have reduced accidents and injuries in the subways, officials who instituted such policies are unlikely to be shy about claiming credit. Nor are most voters likely to inquire about the total number of injuries and deaths during rush hour on all modes of transportation put together. That would require thinking beyond stage one. In short, third-party decision-making, based on categorical reasoning and one-stage thinking, often succeeds in the political arena, even though individual decision-making for oneself is more likely to involve an incremental weighing of benefits against costs. Those skilled in rhetoric can easily ignore hidden costs which those faced with decisions for themselves are more likely to take into account.

There are other situations in which caution—at stage one—can turn out to be dangerous in the long run. Nor are these situations confined to economics. In the American Civil War, for example, General George McClelland's cautious use of the Union army has often been blamed for more fatalities than if he had been more aggressive and not let defeated Confederate troops escape to fight another day. McClelland's insistence on waiting to get his forces organized before launching another attack allowed the Confederates time to both escape and dig in to create stronger defensive positions, from which they could later more readily kill more Union attackers.

Another and more general way in which one kind of safety increases other risks involves the role of wealth. Reconsider the common statement, "If it saves just one life, it is worth whatever it costs." This sacrifice of wealth would make sense only if wealth saved no lives. But, in reality, wealth is one of the biggest life-saving factors, so that sacrificing wealth costs lives, whether that sacrifice takes the form of money spent for safety devices or a reduction in economic efficiency for the sake of risk reduction. Whether any given policy makes sense depends on *how much* risk reduction takes place for how much sacrifice of wealth. Forbidding trucks from driving 100 miles an hour on the highway probably saves more lives than it costs in lost efficiency, but forcing cars to drive under 15 miles an hour may not. In short, decisions about policies designed to produce net savings of lives involve incremental trade-offs, not categorical pronouncements, however attractive those pronouncements may sound.

The role of wealth in saving lives can be dramatic, whether comparing rich and poor in a given society or prosperous nations with Third World nations. An economist in India has pointed out that "95% of deaths from natural hazards occur in poor countries." Since virtually all countries were poorer in the past, this also implies that deaths from natural disasters have been declining over time, for both rich and poor countries. Empirical evidence supports that conclusion.

Six to eight thousand people perished in a hurricane that struck Galveston, Texas, in 1900 but fewer than 50 died when Hurricane Andrew hit Florida in 1992—even though Andrew was the most destructive hurricane ever to hit the United States. Similarly in India where, as Indian economist Barun Mitra put it, a drought in the year 2000 was dubbed the worst of the century by the media, which "struggled to identify even one victim, while quietly forgetting the past famines that cost the lives of millions." Medical, automotive, and other hazards are likewise affected by the wealth of the people and nations where they occur.

"SOCIAL INSURANCE"

Everything that is called insurance is not in fact insurance. In the countries of the European Union, government retirement programs account for 90 percent of all retirement income, often under the name "social insurance." But real insurance is very different from these government pension programs. Real insurance is based on careful mathematical and statistical calculations of risks and of the premiums required to cover those risks. These are known as actuarial calculations and only when the assets of insurance companies cover their liabilities are they said to be actuarially sound. Their assets include both the premiums they have received and their additional earnings from having invested those premiums. Whatever they are obligated by law to pay to their policy-holders are the insurance company's liabilities.

Government-run social insurance programs seldom have enough assets to cover their liabilities, but rely instead on making current payments out of current receipts. These are called pay-as-you-go programs—and sometimes they are also called pyramid schemes. Pyramid schemes are privately run pay-as-you-go plans—and they are illegal because of their high risk of default and the opportunities for those who run them to take part of the money for themselves. The most famous pyramid scheme was run by a man named Charles Ponzi, who went to jail back in 1920. He used the same principles behind the pension plans of many Western governments today.

Ponzi had promised, within 90 days, to double the investment of those who paid into his program. The first investors who were not deterred by warnings from skeptics were in fact rewarded by having their investments pay off double in 90 days. Ponzi simply paid the first wave of investors with money received from the growing second wave of investors, and the second wave from the even larger number of those in the third wave, as enthusiasm for his plan spread. So long as the number of people attracted to this plan formed an expanding pyramid, both the earlier investors and Ponzi profited handsomely. But, once the pyramid stopped growing, there was no way to continue to pay off those who sent Ponzi their money, since his scheme created no new wealth.

The American Social Security pension system and similar government pension systems in the countries of the European Union likewise take in payments from people who are working and use that money to pay the pensions of people who have retired. Unlike Ponzi's pyramid scheme, these government pension plans have much longer than 90 days before the promised pensions are scheduled to be paid. They have decades before they have to redeem the promises of the system to workers after they retire. Moreover, the small generation of people working in the 1930s, when Social Security began in the United States, was succeeded by a much larger "baby boom" generation after World War II, so the pyramid of contributors was predestined to grow. The economies of countries with such programs also grew, allowing working people with much higher incomes to be taxed to cover pensions based on the much lower incomes of the 1930s generation. The promises not only were kept, the benefits were often expanded beyond those promised.

Those who warned that these were essentially Ponzi schemes without enough assets to cover their liabilities—that they were "actuarially unsound" in the financial jargon—were either not believed or were brushed aside for having made objections that were theoretically correct but in practice irrelevant. One of those who brushed these objections aside was Professor Paul Samuelson of MIT, winner of the first Nobel Prize in economics:

> The beauty of social insurance is that it is actuarially unsound. Everyone who reaches retirement age is given benefit privileges that far exceed anything he has paid in . . . Always there are more youths than old folks in a growing population. More important, with real incomes growing at some 3% a year, the taxable base upon which benefits rest in any period are much greater than the taxes paid his-

torically by the generation now retired . . . A growing nation is the
greatest Ponzi game ever contrived.

By the end of the twentieth century, however, the day of reckon-
ing began to loom on the horizon for these government pension
programs, as it had for the original Ponzi scheme. Contrary to
Professor Samuelson's assertion, there are not *always* "more youths
than old folks." As birth rates declined in the Western world and
life expectancy increased, vastly increasing the number of years in
which pensions would have to be paid to more people, it became
painfully clear that either tax rates were going to have to rise by
very large amounts or the benefits would have to be reduced in
one way or another—or both—or the system would simply run
out of money.

In 2002, the credit-rating agency Standard & Poor's calculated
the liabilities representing promised pension benefits to add up to
more than the annual Gross Domestic Product of nine of the 15
European Union nations. These were the kinds of overwhelming
debts usually run up in fighting a major war. Moreover, wars usually end in a few years, so that these debts can begin to be paid off,
while there are endless generations of retirees ahead, living longer
and longer. Demographic projections showed the size of the population of retirement age, compared to the size of the working-age
population, to be rising sharply for the first half of the twenty-first
century, not only in the European Union countries, but in Japan
and the United States as well.

The underlying reason for the crisis atmosphere surrounding
many discussions of how to "save" Social Security in the late twentieth and early twenty-first centuries came from the fact that the
contributions paid by workers were not invested, like insurance
premiums, but spent. Because there was no real fund of wealth to

draw on in pay-as-you-go government pension plans, these plans had the same fatal weakness as the original Ponzi scheme. Yet none of that became obvious in stage one. Decades passed before a financial crisis developed, and even then the reason for the crisis was not obvious to many people. The crisis was often blamed on changing demographics, rather than on those who set up a scheme that could work only so long as demographic trends did not change—even though demographic trends had been known to change many times in the past.

Chapter 6

The Economics of Discrimination

It is painfully obvious that discrimination inflicts economic and other costs on those being discriminated against. What is not so obvious, but is an important causal factor nonetheless, is that discrimination also has a cost to those who do the discriminating. Moreover, the cost of discriminating varies with the circumstances. For an American owner of a professional basketball team to refuse to hire blacks would be to commit financial suicide. But, for the conductor of a symphony orchestra to pass over the relatively few black violinists available would cost practically nothing, in the absence of anti-discrimination laws, since there are far more white violinists available to take their places.

Variations in the costs of discrimination help explain many otherwise puzzling anomalies, such as the fact that blacks were starring on Broadway in the 1920s, at a time when a black man could not enlist in the U. S. Navy nor a black woman be hired as a telephone operator by most phone companies, even in the Northern states. Variations in the cost of discrimination also help explain why black ghettoes in the United States tended to expand with the growth of the black population in the twentieth century, while in centuries past Jewish ghettoes in Europe tended simply to become more overcrowded with the growth of the Jewish population. In countries around the world, employment discrimination has tended to be greatest in the hiring of government employees and employees in government-regulated utilities.

Before getting into the economics behind such things, it is first necessary to be clear as to just what is and is not defined as discrimination, so that we can avoid talking past each other, as happens too often in discussions of discrimination.

PREJUDICE, BIAS, AND DISCRIMINATION

Prejudice, bias, and discrimination are too often confused with one another. Each requires careful definition before discussing substantive issues, if those discussions are not to get hopelessly bogged down in semantics.

Prejudice

Prejudice means pre-judgement. Yet the term has been widely used more loosely to refer to adverse opinions in general about particular racial or ethnic groups. Unless we are prepared to accept as dogma that there cannot possibly be anything about the skills, behavior, or performance of any group, anywhere in the world, which reduces their productivity as workers or their desirability as neighbors, we cannot automatically equate adverse opinions or actions with prejudgments. Too much empirical evidence exists to allow any such dogma to survive scrutiny. For example, per capita consumption of alcohol and rates of alcoholism have varied by some multiple among various groups in the United States and in the Soviet Union, among other places—and the adverse effects of alcohol and alcoholism have been too well documented to require elaboration. Rates of crime, disease and other adverse conditions have likewise varied widely among various groups in countries around the world.

Was it only coincidental that cholera was virtually unknown in American cities before the large-scale arrival of immigrants from Ireland in the nineteenth century—and that cholera epidemics swept primarily through Irish neighborhoods in Boston and Philadelphia? Were the organized crime activities of the Chinese tongs in various countries in Southeast Asia mere "perceptions"? Was the Maharashtrian majority in Bombay simply prejudiced against other Maharashtrians when they preferred to buy from businesses run by people from South India, rather than businesses run by their own compatriots? Is it just racial prejudice which causes *black* taxi drivers in New York to avoid picking up black male passengers at night?

Adverse judgments and actions cannot be automatically attributed to prejudgment. Often those with the most direct knowledge have the most adverse judgments, while those observing from afar—or not observing at all—attribute these adverse judgements and actions to prejudice. By the same token, particular minority groups may be sought out for particular attributes judged favorably, without this being a matter of prejudgment. During the great era of skyscraper-building in the United States, for example, Mohawk Indians were often sought out to work high up on the steel frameworks while the skyscrapers were being built, because of their demonstrated ability to perform their work undistracted by the dangers.

In centuries past, Germans' reputation in mining caused them to be sought out for this work in England, Spain, Norway, Mexico, and the Balkans. Back in the eighteenth century, when Catherine the Great decided that Russia needed to bring in "some merchant people" from other countries, she informed one of her high officials that merchants in other parts of Europe should be issued passports to Russia "not mentioning their nationality and without inquiring into their confession." This was a way of circumventing the ban on the immigration of Jews into Russia, rather than take the politically unpopular step of lifting the ban.

In short, whether judgments or actions toward particular groups are favorable or unfavorable, these actions cannot be automatically equated with prejudgments. Indeed, it is a sweeping prejudgment to do so, especially when those who attribute prejudice to others often have less direct knowledge of the groups in question, at the times in question, than those who made the favorable or unfavorable judgments.

Even when favorable or unfavorable judgments about groups are based on knowledge, judgments of particular individuals from within these groups may be made on the basis of prejudice. As W.E.B. DuBois pointed out about the hiring of blacks in the nineteenth century, "the individual black workman is rated not by his own efficiency, but by the efficiency of a whole group of black fellow workmen which may often be low." Therefore, if white people were to lose their racial prejudices overnight, he said, this would make very little immediate difference in the economic condition of most blacks. According to DuBois, writing in 1898, "some few would be promoted, some few would get new places" but "the mass would remain as they are," until the younger generation began to improve in response to greater job opportunities due to reduced racial barriers.

In short, DuBois saw white employers' adverse judgments of black workers at that time as being generally accurate, though not accurate as regards all individual black workers currently or the potential of black workers in the future. Whatever the empirical validity of his assessments, what is relevant here is that he made the crucial analytical distinction between adverse judgments based on experience and unsubstantiated prejudgments. Moreover, while the lumping together of disparate members of a group can explain why particular individuals from that group earn less than comparable individuals from other groups, such individual disparities cannot explain *group* disparities. For that, the generalization about the group's performance as a whole must be erroneous. Seldom is any serious effort made to demonstrate such group-wide errors. More often, the simple fact that an adverse generalization has been made about a group is taken as itself evidence of prejudice.

Bias

Biases differ from prejudices and there are at least two kinds of bias which also differ from each other.

The first kind of bias is what might be called cognitive bias. The person making judgments or taking actions may not begin with any specific adverse beliefs about a particular group, nor any hostility toward them, but his mode of judgment may cause individuals of equal ability to be ranked differently when they come from one group rather than another. For example, someone who places great weight on how an applicant for a job or college admissions dresses may pass up many highly qualified members of groups that do not put much emphasis on dress or who have different patterns of dressing from those of the evaluator or of other groups being evaluated.

Even in the absence of any adverse prejudgments or negative feelings toward the group in question, such an evaluator may thus systematically undervalue the achievements or potential of individuals from some groups. In addition, circumstances may also generate bias, in addition to human bias. As a scholarly study of India noted:

Aspiring members of previously victimized groups encounter biased expectations, misperceptions of their performance, and cultural bias in selection devices; they suffer from the absence of informal networks to guide them to opportunities, entrenched systems of senior-ity crystallize and perpetuate the results of earlier discriminatory se-lections. Thus norms of non-discrimination in present distributions are insufficient to erase or dislodge the cumulative effects of past discrimination.

This kind of situation is sometimes characterized in the United States as "institutional racism," as distinguished from the inten-tional and overt racial bias of individuals. This kind of cognitive bias can also be present in impersonal criteria drawn up in good faith, and many claims have been made that various mental tests are "culturally biased" in this sense.

Before evaluating such claims, it is necessary to be clear as to what is and is not being alleged. Nor can we simply dismiss criteria which produce adverse results for particular groups as "irrelevant" or substitute plausibility for an empirical test of whatever correla-tion may or may not exist between particular criteria and subse-quent performances. While careful empirical analysis is necessary, that analysis must be preceded by clear definitions of what we do and do not mean by the words being used.

Another and very different kind of bias is based on favoritism for one's own group, which may exist independently of any be-lief, presumption, or bias about inferior abilities in other groups. Indeed, this kind of bias can co-exist with a belief that some other group is not merely equal but superior. This is in fact a phenomenon found in various countries around the world. For example, an advocate of affirmative action programs for Malays in Malaysia declared: "Whatever the Malays could do, the Chi-nese could do better and more cheaply." Nor was he the only leader to see his own group as less capable than other groups in the same society. In Nigeria, preferential hiring of people from the northern part of the country was advocated on grounds that otherwise "the less well educated people of the North will be swamped by the thrusting people of the South." The same has been true of leaders of the Sinhalese in Sri Lanka, Turks in Cyprus, Fijians in Fiji, Lulu in Zaire, and Assamese in India's state of Assam.

A political movement organized to ban Japanese immigration to the United States, early in the twentieth century, sought to do so precisely on the ground that these immigrants were of high ability and formidable competitors:

> We have been accustomed to regard the Japanese as an inferior race, but are now suddenly aroused to our danger. They are not window cleaners and house servants. The Japanese can think, can learn, can invent. We have suddenly awakened to the fact that they are gaining a foothold in every skilled industry in our country. They are our equal in intellect; their ability to labor is equal to ours. They are proud, valiant, and courageous, but they can underlive us. . . . We are here today to prevent that very competition.

The bias of those seeking favoritism for themselves is wholly independent of any claim that others are inferior and is often insisted upon most fervently when others are considered to have superior performance. There may of course also be favoritism for groups who consider themselves superior—whites in the American South during the Jim Crow era, whites in South Africa under apartheid, or Germans under the Nazis—but such a belief is not inherent in programs of favoritism, which are perfectly compatible with the opposite belief that others are too formidable as competitors to be dealt with without some offsetting official advantage.

Discrimination

Both bias and prejudice are attitudes. The practical question is how and to what extent such attitudes are translated into acts of discrimination. But before addressing that question, we must first be clear as to what we mean by the word "discrimination."

Policies of treating members of particular groups less favorably than similar members of other groups are usually called "discrimination" when practiced by the group with dominant political power and "reverse discrimination" or "affirmative action" when practiced *against* members of the group with dominant political power. Discrimination may also be practiced by private employers, landlords, or institutions. However, if words are to have any fixed meanings—without which discussions are fruitless—the term cannot be extended to all situations in which some groups turn out to have less favorable outcomes than others.

While biases and prejudices are conditions in people's minds, discrimination is an overt act taking place outside their minds in the real world. Nor is there necessarily a one-to-one correlation between the two, as so often assumed by those who make the fight against "racism" their number one priority or by those who claim that opponents of affirmative action must be assuming that prejudice and bias have been eradicated.

It is not only theoretically possible to have more discrimination where there is less bias or prejudice, and less discrimination where there is more bias and prejudice, this has in fact happened in more than one country. The degree to which subjective attitudes are translated into overt acts of discrimination depends on the *costs* of doing so. Where those costs are very high, even very prejudiced or biased people may engage in little or no discrimination. One need only imagine the owner of a professional basketball team who has deeply racist beliefs but even deeper commitments to making money. The first black football player signed by the Washington Redskins in the 1960s was hired by a man reputed among sports writers who knew him to be deeply racist. Yet he broke a long tradition of all-white football teams in Washington by hiring a top running back who was black, at a time when most of the leading running backs in the league were black—and when the Redskins' running game was very ineffective.

There is no inherent contradiction in a racist breaking the color line to hire blacks—or in someone who is not a racist failing to do so. The costs they face when making their decisions must be taken into account, along with their predispositions, in any causal analysis. During the last years of the Jim Crow era in the South, there were stories of Southerners like Arkansas' Senator J. William Fulbright who voted against their consciences to continue racial segregation, because to do otherwise would be to jeopardize their political careers. Personal costs can lead to actions either more adverse or less adverse than the individual's own beliefs and feelings.

VARIATIONS IN COSTS

Where the costs of discrimination are low or non-existent for those making hiring and promotions decisions, then discrimination can become extensive, not only in terms of decisions not to hire or promote members of particular groups, but also in terms of extending such discrimination to a wider range of groups.

At one time, there were said to be American railroads in which Catholics could rise only so high and others in which this was true of Protestants. Within living memory, there was a time when not a single Ivy League college or university had a Jew among its tenured faculty, despite a large number of Jewish intellectuals and scholars available. Nor was a black allowed in the Marine Corps, at even the lowliest rank, when World War II began. In other parts of the world as well, there has been similarly severe discrimination, sometimes even broader in its scope.

While many discussions of discriminations ignore the *cost* of discrimination to those doing the discriminating, on the most elementary economic principle that more is demanded at a lower price than at a higher price, we should expect to see the severity of discrimination vary with the cost to the discriminator. That is in fact what we find in country after country and in era after era—but only if we look at evidence.

In Poland between the two world wars, for example, an absolute majority of all the physicians in the country were from the Jewish minority, which was only 6 percent of the population. Yet the Polish government did not hire Jewish physicians, though many other Poles obviously became patients of Jewish physicians in the private sector, or else so many Jewish doctors could not have made a living. What was the difference between the public sector and the private sector in this regard?

In both sectors, there were both financial and medical costs to refusing to use Jewish physicians. To staff a government hospital with all-Gentile physicians, in a country where such physicians were in the minority in that profession, meant either having to pay more to attract a disproportionate share of the available Gentile physicians or accepting lesser-qualified physicians than some of those available from the Jewish community. In either case, financial or medical costs were entailed, if not both. However, in the case of those who made decisions within the Polish government, there was no cost at all to be paid by them. Financial costs were paid by the taxpayers and the human costs were paid by patients in government hospitals, subject to lower quality medical treatment than was available in the society at the time. Neither of these costs was a deterrent to discrimination by government officials.

In the private sector, both kinds of costs were paid by sick people. Concern for one's own personal health, especially in an emergency situation or when confronted with a potentially crippling or fatal disease, could easily overcome whatever anti-Jewish attitudes one might have. Given the respective incentives in the government and private sectors, the different levels of discrimination against Jews is very much what one might expect, on the basis of the most elementary economic principles.

Poland provides examples of another phenomenon—more discrimination where there was less hostility and less discrimination where there was more hostility. Anti-Jewish feelings tended to be stronger in eastern Poland than in western Poland. Yet Jewish artisans were more prevalent in eastern Poland, just as black artisans once had better job opportunities in the American South, where racism was most rampant. In both cases, organized labor affected the cost of discrimination.

Guilds were stronger in western Poland than in eastern Poland and American labor unions were stronger in the North than in the South during the eras under discussion. To the extent that organized labor succeeds in raising pay levels above where they would be under supply and demand in a free market, they provide incentives for employers to hire fewer workers because labor is now more costly, both absolutely and relative to the cost of capital that may be substituted for it. At the same time, wage rates raised above the level that would prevail under supply and demand attract more workers who apply for jobs that have higher pay. The net effect is that organized labor tends to create a surplus of job applicants. Given that surplus, the cost to the employer of turning away qualified applicants from the "wrong" group is less than it would be if he had to be concerned about finding enough similarly qualified replacements for those who have been arbitrarily rejected.

Even in the absence of discrimination by guilds or unions themselves—and there was plenty of that—it would still be cheaper for employers to discriminate on their own. Given this situation, it is not so puzzling that Jewish artisans found it easier to practice their skills in that part of Poland that was more hostile to Jews and that black American artisans found it easier to practice their skills in the Jim Crow South than in the more unionized North. Differences in costs of discrimination outweighed differences in hostile predispositions.

The same pattern can be seen in employment statistics over time. Both in the American South during the Jim Crow era and in South Africa under white rule, blacks were a much higher percentage of railroad employees in the early twentieth century than they were at mid-century. In both countries, labor markets were more freely competitive in the earlier era and more controlled in the later era—and in both countries it would be hard to claim that there was less racism in the earlier era.

Not only labor unions, but also government regulation, can reduce the cost of discrimination. Where a public utility with a monopoly has its prices set by a government regulatory agency on the basis of its costs, it has little or no incentive to keep those costs down to a level that would be necessary for its survival in a competitive market. Costs of discrimination, like other costs, can simply be passed on to the customers of a regulated monopoly. When the American telephone industry was a regulated monopoly, few blacks were hired for even such routine jobs as telephone operators before the civil rights laws were enacted. Because each local telephone company was a monopoly within its own territory, it could pass on higher costs to everyone who used telephones. Had it not discriminated, its costs would be lower and its monopoly profits could theoretically have been higher, but because its profit rates were in fact constrained by government regulation, the phone company would never have seen that additional money anyway. Instead, it could indulge its racial preferences with no net loss of profits.

Meanwhile, blacks were beginning to star on Broadway as early as the 1920s, in an industry with cut-throat competition, where large profits and devastating losses were both common. The cost of refusing to hire black entertainers who could fill a theater was just too high for this industry to follow the same practices as the telephone industry. The one-to-one correspondence between racism and discrimination that is often assumed cannot explain such differences between sectors of the same economy at the same time. Even less can it explain the persistence of such differences over time, when there is a complete turnover of decision-makers throughout the economy. Even after a given set of decision-makers and their individual predispositions have passed from the scene, the persistence of the same set of incentives tends to reproduce the same end results with a new set of decision-makers in the same respective industries, whatever the individual predispositions of these new decision-makers.

Because major league baseball operated as a cartel exempted from anti-trust laws, it too had low costs of discrimination and was able to keep black players out—so long as all teams did so.

But this situation changed in 1947, when the Brooklyn Dodgers hired Jackie Robinson as the first black major league ballplayer. Because there was competition *within* the cartel among its various teams, once the color barrier was broken by just one team hiring just one black player, the cost to other teams of keeping out other black players rose sharply. The net result was that, in a matter of a relatively few years, large numbers of black players flooded into the major leagues. For a period of seven consecutive years, no white man won the National League's Most Valuable Player award. Had other teams not followed the lead of the Dodgers in hiring black players, all these MVP stars would have become Dodgers, giving Brooklyn a virtual monopoly of National League pennants and perhaps of world championships.

This cost was obviously much too high for the competing teams to pay for continuing racial exclusion in major league baseball. Their racial attitudes may not have changed, but the cost of translating those attitudes into discriminatory exclusions had changed drastically.

Given the influence of the costs of discrimination on the amount of actual discrimination, it is also possible to understand another otherwise puzzling phenomenon—the especially strong reversals of racial policies in sectors of the economy least subject to the pressures of the competitive marketplace. These include the government itself, government-regulated public utilities, and non-profit organizations, such as academic institutions, hospitals, and foundations. Colleges and universities that had never hired blacks for their faculties in pre-World War II America led the way when affirmative action in the 1960s and 1970s meant preferential hiring and promotion of black professors and preferential admissions of black students. There was also a very similar sharp reversal of hiring policies in the telephone industry, among others, at the same time.

These sudden radical changes from especially discriminatory policies against a particular group to preferential policies toward the very same group are hard to explain by predispositions, since many of the same decision-makers were in control during the transition period. It is much easier to understand in terms of the incentives and constraints of the circumstances in which they operated. More specifically, neither discrimination nor "reverse discrimination" cost them as much as either policy would have cost decision-makers in those sectors of the economy where institutional survival depends on keeping costs within narrow limits, in order to meet competition in a free market. Once the political and social climate changed, government, government-regulated utilities, and non-profit organizations could change most quickly with the least cost to themselves.

The power of the free market was perhaps best demonstrated in white-ruled South Africa during the era of apartheid. Here we need not wonder about racial predispositions or about the fact that the vast majority of employers in industry, agriculture, and government were white. Yet, even in a country which became a worldwide symbol of racial oppression, white employers in competitive industries violated official government policy on a massive scale by hiring more black workers and in higher positions than the law allowed. There is no compelling evidence that these particular white employers had different racial predispositions than the white people who administered the apartheid government. What they had were very different costs of discrimination.

While government agencies and government-regulated railroads, for example, could maintain apartheid policies at virtually zero cost to themselves, it was a wholly different economic situation for people spending their own money. Home-building was a typical example:

> To build a house in Johannesburg meant either waiting for months for a white, expensive, legal building gang, or finding a black gang, perhaps with a white nominally in charge in case an official came inquiring. Most customers opted for the quicker, cheaper service.

Such practices became so widespread in South Africa that the white-run apartheid government cracked down in the 1970s, fining hundreds of building construction companies. Moreover, this was by no means the only industry that hired more blacks than they were allowed to by law. In the Transvaal clothing industry, no blacks at all were allowed to work, under the apartheid laws. Yet, as of 1969, blacks were an absolute majority of the workers in that industry. There were also residential areas in South Africa set aside by law for whites only—and yet there were not only many non-whites living in these areas (including black American econo-

mist Walter Williams), at least one such area had an absolute majority of non-whites. Competition in a free market simply made
discrimination too expensive for many, even though violating the
apartheid laws also cost money.[1]

The expansion of black residential areas into white residential areas has been even more common in the United States. However, this
more or less continuous expansion of black ghettoes has been in
contrast to the history of the original ghettoes—those of the Jews in
Europe in centuries past. Jewish ghettoes in Europe in centuries past
tended to become more overcrowded as the Jewish population grew,
though there were particular times and places where Jews were allowed to expand an existing ghetto or to set up a new ghetto to accommodate their growing populations. Here again, the difference
has been in the economic costs of discrimination.

Black ghettoes have expanded through the marketplace because
of the costs of excluding black renters and home buyers. This is not
to say that there was no resistance by whites. Often there was organized, bitter, and even violent resistance. The key question, however, is: What was the end result? The usual end result was that
black ghettoes expanded in cities across the country. Moreover,
where this expansion was stopped by laws or government policies,
by restrictive covenants, or by violence or the threat of violence,
that reinforces the point that the costs of discrimination were too
great for the expansion of black ghettoes to be stopped in the marketplace. By and large, black ghettoes continued expanding with
the growth of the black population.

---

[1]One of the reasons for the weakening of apartheid, even before the end of white-minority rule in
South Africa, was that many of the white Afrikaners, the principal supporters of apartheid, rose over
the years into the ranks of business owners and now had to pay the costs of discrimination, which
had been paid by British and Jewish business owners before. Faced with these costs, many Afrikaners began to lose their enthusiasm for apartheid and some even spoke out against it, despite the
authoritarian South African government.

The boundaries of Jewish ghettoes in Europe were not determined by the marketplace but were established by the dictates of those with political power. Only when these political leaders found it expedient did these boundaries expand. That is why Jewish ghettoes tended simply to become more crowded with the passage of time and population growth. There was usually no cost to political leaders for discriminating against Jews. In particular circumstances—when there was a war on, for example, and the rulers needed the help of Jewish financiers—various proscriptions might be eased and more ghettoes allowed to be founded to relieve overcrowding. During the Thirty Years War (1618–1648), for example, new Jewish communities were permitted to be established and new occupations and markets opened up to Jews, while a synagogue was permitted to be built in Vienna for the first time in more than 200 years and a synagogue was permitted in Denmark for the first time ever.

In short, costs of discrimination are not only a fact of life, they are a potent force in actual decision-making, even in countries with strong racial, ethnic, or religious predispositions. How much of a force depends on the economic incentives and constraints in particular sectors. What this means is that not only is the assumed one-to-one correlation between racism and discrimination false, but also that those who wish to reduce discrimination need to pay attention to the economic conditions which make it more expensive or less expensive for decision-makers to discriminate. Too often, those opposed to discrimination are also opposed to free competitive markets that make discrimination more costly. They do not think beyond stage one.

Even a given market—such as the market for housing, for example—can have more discrimination or less discrimination according to whether its prices are detemined by supply and demand or are imposed by external agencies such as government, labor unions, or a cartel. For example, when a landlord refuses to rent an apartment to people from the "wrong" group, that can mean leaving the apartment vacant longer. Clearly, that represents a loss of rent—if this is a free market. However, if there is rent control, with a surplus of applicants, then such discrimination may cost the landlord nothing.

Similar principles apply in job markets. An employer who refuses to hire qualified individuals from the "wrong" groups risks leaving his jobs unfilled longer in a free market. This means that he must either leave some work undone and some orders unfilled or else pay overtime to existing employees to get it done, losing money either way. However, in a market where wages are set artificially above the level that would exist through supply and demand, the resulting surplus of applicants can mean that discrimination costs the employer nothing. Whether these artificially higher wages are set by a labor union or by a minimum wage law does not change the principle.

In all these cases, the crucial factors in the cost of discrimination have been the presence or absence of competition and whether those making the decisions have been spending their own money or someone else's money. When one's own money is at stake, groups hostile to each other may not only fail to discriminate, they may in fact seek each other out, as Polish immigrants and Jewish immigrants from Poland did in early twentieth-century Chicago:

> . . . the Poles and the Jews in Chicago . . . have a profound feeling of disrespect and contempt for each other, bred by contiguity and by historical friction in the pale; but they trade with each other on Milwaukee Avenue and on Maxwell Street. A study of numerous cases shows that not only do many Jews open their businesses on Milwaukee Avenue and Division Street because they know that the Poles

are the predominant population in these neighborhoods, but the Poles come from all over the city to trade on Maxwell Street because they know that there they can find the familiar street-stands owned by Jews.

EMPIRICAL EVIDENCE

Those who equate discrimination with differences in life chances confound highly disparate reasons for differences in outcomes among groups. Even if one regards differences in life chances as more important than discrimination, any serious attempt to deal with either social phenomenon must distinguish them from one another.

Life Chances

In one sense, life chances are easier to determine than discrimination. For the past, the probabilities that a black child would become a physician or a member of Congress can be determined mathematically from statistics on the size of the black population and the numbers of blacks who ended up in those occupations. Even in this simplest case, however, there are complications.

Do we mean by life chances mere statistical probabilities in general or do we mean the likelihood that a given attempt, with a given effort, will succeed? What if very few black boys want to become ballet dancers or are prepared to endure peer disapproval if they persist in their efforts in this direction? In short, even the apparently simple issue of determining life chances raises complicating questions as to the *source* of the differences in probabilities and outcomes among groups. Whether that source is internal or external becomes even more of a complication when seeking to determine the existence and magnitude of discrimination.

Where discrimination is distinguished from differences in life chances, the empirical question is whether individuals of similar qualifications have similar prospects of employment, college admission, and other benefits when they come from different groups.

Where there are substantial differences in qualifying characteristics among groups, as there often are, the question then becomes: What of those particular individuals who have the same qualifying characteristics as members of other groups? Do they have the same prospects or results?

Comparability

Gross comparisons between groups may tell a radically different story than comparisons of comparable individuals. For example, black income has never been as high as white income in the United States and, in years past, the disparities were even greater than they are today. Yet, as far back as 1969, young black males who came from homes where there were newspapers, magazines, and library cards earned the same incomes as young white males with the same things in their homes and with the same education. As of 1989, black, white, and Hispanic Americans of the same age (29) and with the same IQ (100) all averaged between $25,000 and $26,000 in income when they worked year around.

American women's incomes have never been as high as the incomes of American men but, as early as 1971, women in their thirties who had never married and who had worked continuously since high school earned slightly *higher* incomes than men of the same description. In Canada, women who never married have earned more than 99 percent of the income of men who never married. Among college faculty members, American women who had never married earned substantially *higher* incomes than men who had never married, as far back as 1969.

None of this says anything about life chances, however relevant it may be to questions about employer discrimination. The percentage of black males who came from the kinds of homes described was very different from the percentage of white males who came from such homes. IQ scores are likewise distributed very differently among American blacks, whites, and Hispanics. It is not uncommon, both in the United States and in other countries, for one racial or ethnic group to differ in age from another by a decade or more—and age makes a large difference in income. So does marriage. While married men tend to earn more than single men and married men with children still more, the exact opposite is the case for women. Nor are the reasons particularly obscure, since marriage and parenthood create very different incentives and constraints for women than for men.

The justice or social desirability of traditional sex roles in marriage can be debated. But that debate is not about employer discrimination, much less about the presumed predispositions of employers. Questions about the existence or magnitude of employer discrimination are questions about whether individuals who show up at the workplace with the same developed capabilities and liabilities are treated the same there. It is not a question about whether life has been fair to them before they reached the employer, however important that question might be when dealing with other issues. Yet, increasingly, laws and policies have defined as employer discrimination a failure to pay the extra costs associated with those workers who are pregnant, suffering from mental illness, or are more of a risk because of a prison record or the health problems associated with old age. When hiring, employers have incentives to think beyond stage one, even if those who make or advocate laws and government policies do not.

Whatever the merits or demerits of having such additional costs paid by the employer or by the government or by others, a failure to do so is not the same thing as treating equally valuable workers differently because they happen to come from different groups. When workers whose net value to the enterprise are in fact different are hired, paid and promoted according to those differences, that is not employer discrimination, whatever else it might be. This is not even a question about desirable social policy. It is a question about using words that have some specific meaning, rather than as mere sounds to evoke particular emotions. Only when terms have some specific meaning, understood by those on both sides of an issue, can we at least engage in rational discussions of our differences of opinion about what is or is not desirable social policy. Otherwise, we are simply talking past each other.

While isolated data can demonstrate graphically the distinction between differing life chances, on the one hand, and discrimination on the other, the more general problem of determining which phenomenon exists in particular situations requires more complex and often uncertain methods. For example, it is common to "control" statistically for certain factors and then see if individuals from different groups have similar results when those factors have been taken into consideration. Yet this is much easier to accept in principle than to apply in practice.

Nothing is easier than to imagine that one has taken all relevant factors into account, when in reality there may be other factors which have influence, even if no data have been collected on them or they are not quantifiable. Where there are very significant differences in known factors between one group and another, it would be reckless to assume that all remaining unknown factors are the same. Yet that is done again and again in discussions of discrimination.

A scholar in India, for example, attempted to compare Bombay medical school students with such comparable social characteristics as father's income and occupation, but later discovered in the course of interviewing these students that those who were the same in these respects, but who were also untouchables, were not comparable on other variables, such as the quality of the schools they had come from, the number of books in the homes in which they had grown up, and the literacy rates among their fathers and grandfathers.

Similarly, a study of black and white faculty members in the United States found that those who were comparable on some variables were nevertheless very different on other variables. Even black professors with Ph.D.s usually received those Ph.D.s at a later age, from institutions with lower rankings in their respective fields, and these professors had published fewer articles. When such variables as published articles, the ranking of the institutions from which Ph.D.s were earned, and years of academic experience were all held constant, black professors with Ph.D.s earned *more* than white professors with Ph.D.s, as far back as 1970—a year before affirmative action policies were mandated by the federal government.

None of this is unusual. It is commonplace in countries around the world for groups who differ in the quantity of their education to differ also in the quality of their education. This means that comparisons of individuals with ostensibly the "same" education from different groups can amount to comparisons of apples and oranges. Therefore equating differences in pay between members of different groups who have the "same" education with discrimination is a non sequitur.

Educational quality may differ along many dimensions, including institutional ranking, individual performance, or fields of specialization. Such differences have existed between the Chinese and the Malays in Malaysia, Tamils and Sinhalese in Sri Lanka, and European and American Jews versus Middle Eastern Jews in Israel, as well as between caste Hindus and untouchables in India and among blacks, whites, and Hispanics in the United States. The education of American college-educated women and men likewise differs in fields of specialization and in the postgraduate education added on to that of these women and men whose education is considered the "same" because they have all graduated from college.

Education is not unique in having such differences among apparently similar individuals from different groups. A highly publicized study which concluded that there was racial discrimination between minority and white applicants for mortgage loans in the United States failed to note that the minority applicants had larger debts, poorer credit histories, sought loans covering a higher percentage of the value of the properties in question, and were also more likely to seek to finance multiple dwelling units rather than single-family homes.

When these factors were taken into account, the differences in mortgage loan approval rates shrank dramatically, though the remaining difference of 6 percentage points was nevertheless attributed to discrimination, as if there could not possibly be any other differences in the remaining unstudied factors, despite large differences in the variables that were already studied. For example, other data from the U.S. Census show that blacks and whites with the same incomes average very different net worths—and net worth is also a major consideration in decisions to approve or disapprove mortgage loan applications.

Much statistical data does not permit such a fine breakdown as the data comparing black and white faculty members in 1970 or the follow-up study on mortgage lending. For much of the media—and often even in academia—it is sufficient to find intergroup differences in outcomes to conclude that there has been discrimination. This happens, however, only when the conclusion fits existing preconceptions. Statistics showing Asian-Americans to have higher incomes, lower infant mortality rates, and higher rates of mortgage application approval than white Americans are never taken to show discrimination against whites, even though identical data—often from the same studies—are taken as proof of discrimination against blacks.

Gross statistical differences between the "representation" of different groups in particular occupations, institutions, or income levels are likewise usually considered sufficient for concluding that the "under-represented" groups were "excluded" by discriminatory policies or by individual or institutional biases or prejudices, however subtle, covert or unconscious these might be. Yet nothing is more common, in countries around the world, than huge differences in representation between groups, even when the more fortunate group is in no position to discriminate against the less fortunate group. These include situations where the more fortunate group is a minority with no institutional or political power over the majority.

In Malaysia, for example, for the entire decade of the 1960s, members of the Chinese minority in Malaysia received more than 400 degrees in engineering, while members of the Malay majority received just four. This was in a country where the universities were controlled by the Malays, who also controlled the government that controlled the universities.

Nor was this situation unique. In czarist Russia, the German minority—about one percent of the population—was an absolute majority in the St. Petersburg Academy of Science. Jewish physicians were an absolute majority of all physicians in Poland and Hungary in the period between the two World Wars, though Jews were less than 12 percent of the population in both countries. Southern Nigerians were an absolute majority of the people in a number of professions in northern Nigeria when that country gained its independence. The list could go on and on, filling a book much larger than this one.

None of this disproves the existence of discrimination or mini-
mizes its magnitude. It simply asks that those who assert its existence *demonstrate* its existence—by some evidence that will stand
up to scrutiny.

ANTI-DISCRIMINATION LAWS

Both discrimination and affirmative action involve costs. It could
hardly be otherwise, since they are both essentially preferential
policies, though the preferences are for different groups. Whatever
the rationales or goals of these policies, the economic question is:
What are the actual consequences of such policies—and not just in
stage one? In principle, anti-discrimination laws are a third policy,
designed to preclude preferential treatment of either a majority or
minority. But this policy as well cannot be defined by its intentions, goals or rationales. The real question is: What are its specific
characteristics and their consequences—and, again, not just in
stage one?

The likely consequences of laws and policies against discrimination depend on how discrimination is defined and determined by
those with the power to enforce such laws and policies. The incentives and constraints created by these definitions and methods of determining whether or not discrimination exists provide more clues
as to what to expect than do the goals or rationales. What is then
decisive is the empirical evidence as to what actually happens.

Legal Definitions

In the United States, "discrimination" had a very simple and
straightforward legal meaning at the beginning of the federal
civil rights legislation of the 1960s. It meant treating individuals
differently according to the racial or ethnic group in which they

were classified. Even the term "affirmative action," as used initially in President John F. Kennedy's Executive Order in 1961, meant that an employer must be active, rather than passive, to make sure that job applicants and employees were treated the same, "without regard to their race, creed, color or national origin." Anti-discrimination laws, such as the Civil Rights Act of 1964, were likewise designed to prevent differential treatment in employment, in access to public accommodations, and in various other contexts. However, even before the Civil Rights Act of 1964 was passed, a competing definition of discrimination had already begun to emerge.

Earlier that year, a state Fair Employment Practices Commission in Illinois ruled that the Motorola company had discriminated against a black job applicant by requiring him to take the same test that other applicants took. This was considered to be discriminatory because blacks usually did not have either as much or as good an education as whites, and so were less likely to do well on tests. As one of the Commission's examiners put it, the test was "unfair to culturally deprived and disadvantaged groups." This implicitly shifted the operational definition of discrimination from a denial of equal treatment to a denial of equal prospects of success.

Critics of the federal civil rights legislation being considered in Congress pointed to the Motorola case as an example of what to expect if the Civil Rights Act of 1964 became law, while the Act's advocates and defenders vehementaly denied it. Although nothing in the Act itself authorized any such definition of discrimination, subsequent interpretations by the federal courts, including the Supreme Court, established the broader definition of discrimination as the use of criteria which have a "disparate impact" on the prospects of success by minority groups. In other words, a failure to have a workforce reflecting the demographic profile of the local community was now taken as presumptive evidence of discrimination, with the burden of proof to the contrary falling on the employer.

The issues revolving around such policies have already been amply—or perhaps more than amply—debated by many advocates and critics from political, moral, legal, and sociological perspectives. The economic question, however, is: What incentives and constraints does this definition of discrimination create and what are the likely consequences of those incentives and constraints?

Economic Consequences

The most obvious and most immediate consequence is that those employers who were discriminating against minorities now had an incentive to stop doing so, in order to avoid the costs arising from legal action under anti-discrimination laws. However, the empirical evidence suggests that the extent of discrimination in the sense of treating equally capable individuals differently because of race, may have been considerably less than that assumed by those who equate discrimination with different outcomes for different groups. Nevertheless, whether the amount of discrimination is large or small, the immediate, stage-one effect of anti-discrimination laws is to reduce it.

What about other consequences unfolding over time? The ease with which private parties or government agencies can make a charge of discrimination against an employer who is in fact not discriminating, but whose work force does not reflect the local population profile, now makes locating near concentrations of minority populations legally more risky. Those employers in these risky locations may not be able to do much about it in the short run. However, as time goes on, new businesses that arise have a choice of where to locate and even old businesses with branches in more than one location can shift their operations away from minority population centers, in order to reduce their legal risks. Eventually, even the employer with only one plant or office can find an opportunity to move elsewhere.

Whether minority workers gain more jobs through the effect of anti-discrimination laws in reducing discrimination or lose more jobs through the incentives that such laws provide for employers to relocate is an empirical question. But it is a question that is seldom asked.

For the employer, one way of avoiding charges of discrimination by minority employees or job applicants may be to hire in such a way as to have a racially representative sample of the local population. However, this can risk charges of "reverse discrimination" by white job applicants who were not hired, or white employees who were passed over for promotion. Since racial or ethnic groups tend to differ in their particular skills and experience, it is unlikely that the qualifications of members of different groups in a given location will be the same—the only way to have both non-discriminatory hiring and a demographically representative workforce at the same time.

One way out of this dilemma for many employers is to hire in such a way as to create demographic representation, and at the same time escape charges of "reverse discrimination," is to justify preferential hiring on grounds of affirmative action based on a need for "diversity." This legal avoidance of lawsuits from both minority and majority individuals, or government agencies, works only in so far as courts accept such arguments. Therefore, when affirmative action has been challenged in the Supreme Court, even when it is challenged in cases involving college admissions, many corporations have filed briefs in favor of the colleges with racial preferences in admissions standards. The principle involved is a legal safe haven for employers, and one which they do not want to lose.

IMPLICATIONS

Much discussion of discrimination fails to allow people with opposing views to confront their substantive differences—much less confront evidence—because so many of the words used have ambiguous and shifting meanings. In particular, these discussions abound in terms which confuse differences in internal personal qualities—such as skills, education, and experience—with externally imposed barriers to employment, college admissions, and other desired goals. Thus those who fail to qualify for particular benefits are often said to be denied "access" or "opportunity," when in fact they may have had as much access or opportunity as anyone else, but simply did not have the developed capabilities required.

The facts may of course vary from individual to individual or from group to group, but we do not even know what facts to look for when considering issues revolving around discrimination if our terms make no such distinctions. Similarly, a mental test may be characterized as "culturally biased" if one group scores higher than another, as if it is impossible for different groups to have different interest, experience, upbringing, education, or other factors that would lead to a real difference being registered, rather than a mere biased assessment being made.[2]

Would anyone consider basketball to be a culturally biased game because blacks generally play it better than whites? It might well be that, if whites took as much interest in the game and played it as often as blacks, they would be just as good at it. But measuring what people actually do in the real world is very different from as-

---

[2]A complicating factor here is a history of controversies over whether there are innate racial differences in intelligence. But that explosive emotional issue has little or no relevance to questions about discrimination. Innate potential exists at the moment of conception but no one applies for a job or for college admissions at the moment of conception. By the time any such application is made, numerous personal and social factors have had an influence over the years—and these factors have seldom been the same for every individual or for every group. Moreover, employers are far more likely to be interested in the developed capabilities that have emerged, rather than the innate potential with which someone began life.

sessing what they would do under other, hypothetical circumstances. Nor is the owner of a professional basketball team engaging in racial discrimination when he hires more blacks than whites in a country where the population has more whites than blacks.

None of this says anything about how much discrimination there is. What it says is that a vocabulary has come into being that makes it virtually impossible to determine how much discrimination there is, since the results of both discrimination and numerous other factors are lumped together under the same words. Those who do not think beyond stage one may assume that, whatever the level of discrimination, anti-discrimination laws reduce it. Yet the incentives and constraints created by such laws can either increase or reduce the employment or other opportunities of minority groups, on net balance.

There may be honest differences of opinion on what the net balance turns out to be, but even the question itself does not arise until we look beyond stage one. More precise definitions of terms or finer breakdowns of statistics might yield very different estimates of the amount of discrimination, but the crucial point here is that the vocabulary actually in use is not adapted to discovering how much discrimination exists, however well adapted it may be for political purposes.

Chapter 7

The Economic Development of Nations

> Before 1886 there was not one cocoa tree in British West Africa. By the 1930s there were millions of acres under cocoa there, all owned and operated by Africans.
>
> —*Peter Bauer*

All over the world, national economies have generally advanced in recent centuries, producing more output per capita and thereby raising people's standards of living. This advance in technology and wealth has been greater in some regions of the world than in others, and greater during some periods of history than in others. However, there have also been periods of stagnation and periods of retrogression, sometimes brought on by the disruptions and destruction of war, sometimes by plagues or other natural disasters, and sometimes by ill-conceived economic policies.

At the beginning of the twentieth century, Argentina was one of the ten richest countries in the world, ahead of France and Germany. But, at the beginning of the twenty-first century, no one would even compare the troubled and chaotic Argentine economy with that of France or Germany. Many ill-conceived policies in between led to this falling behind in a country blessed with natural resources and spared the wars which ravaged other countries in the twentieth century. Between 1998 and 2002, income per person in Argentina dropped by two-thirds.[1]

Sharp changes in countries' relative positions have taken place in much shorter periods than a century. As of 1991, India and China had very similar output per capita. But, a decade later, China's output per capita was double that of India. China had begun the process of moving away from a government-run economy to more of a market economy. When India began making the same kinds of changes in the 1990s, its economic development became more rapid as well.

While economic development has been more or less taken for granted in much of the Western world since the industrial revolution of the eighteenth and nineteenth centuries, this has not been so in all places and all times—and it was not so in the West for many centuries before then. In some other parts of the world, even in the twentieth century, farmers continued to farm and fishermen continued to fish in much the same way as their ancestors had centuries earlier, leading to standards of living not very different from what they had been in ancient times.

In short, economic development has never been automatic. Why it has been greater in some places than in others, and at some times rather than others, is a question of great practical importance for the economic fate of billions of human beings today, though it is a question for which no single answer is likely to explain everything. Technology has had much to do with it, though not everything. Similarly for geography, natural resources, and other factors, including the hu-

[1]Anthony Faiola, "In Argentina, Dignity Turns to Despair," *The Washington Post National Weekly Edition*, August 17–18, 2002, p. 16.

man factor. As in other areas of economics, attempts to understand certain basic realities are made more difficult by the distractions of popular myths and misconceptions.

DIFFERENCES IN DEVELOPMENT

The striking and even shocking differences in economic development seen in many parts of the contemporary world have led many to develop, or be drawn to, sweeping and often melodramatic theories that claim to explain such economic contrasts. Yet such economic contrasts have been common throughout history. Ancient China was so far in advance of Europe that, while there was a great demand among Europeans for silk, chinaware (the name is significant) and other exotic products, the Europeans produced nothing comparable to trade and so had to pay in gold for what they bought from China. Within Europe, the contrasts have been equally great. When the ancient Greeks had monumental architecture that is still imitated today and landmark intellectual figures like Plato and Aristotle, illiteracy was common across much of northern Europe and there was not a single building in all of Britain when the Romans invaded in the second century A.D., nor had a single Briton's name yet entered the pages of history. The contrast today between the wealth of Western countries and the poverty of the Third World is nothing new.

While differences in economic development have long been common, the particular advantages of one society over another during a particular era have not been permanent. Europe eventually overtook China, after many centuries. So did Japan. More important, the advances achieved in one society have often diffused outward to other societies. What was perhaps the greatest economic advance in the history of the human race—agriculture—began in the Middle East and spread outward, as cultivators of the soil began to displace hunters and gatherers wherever the two competed for the same territory. Agriculture would support far more people on a given amount of land, leading to larger societies with more fighting men than in societies of people who lived by hunting and gathering the spontaneous produce of the earth, and who were necessarily spread more thinly over the land, in order for everyone to have enough to eat.

One society was not always more advanced in all things, so different advances came from different places, even at a given time. For example, the numbering system in use around the world today originated centuries ago among the Hindus of India, and displaced Roman numerals in the West, as well as every other numbering system that it competed with in every other country. Because Europeans first became aware of this numbering system when they encountered it in use among the Arabs, they called such numbers "Arabic numerals." But that was not the origin of these numbers.

Innumerable borrowings from one culture to another have taken place almost continuously over thousands of years. However, the pace of these borrowings and the opportunities to borrow have varied greatly in different parts of the world and in different periods of time. People living in remote mountain valleys or on isolated islands in the middle of a vast sea have usually not been able to keep up with the advances of technology and other developments in other societies. When the Spaniards discovered the Canary Islands in the fifteenth century, they found people of a Caucasian race living at a stone age level. So were the Australian aborigines when the British discovered them. In both cases, isolation meant deprivation of the advances of the human race around the world.

While such things as technology and natural resources are obvious factors in economic development, less obvious factors may be of equal or greater importance. The role of government can be crucial. After the Roman Empire collapsed in the fifth century A.D., the institutions it had maintained collapsed with it. What had once been an inter-connected economy and legal system, stretching from Britain to North Africa, now fragmented into many independent local jurisdictions, often separated by areas of varying sizes that were not effectively controlled by any government and were unsafe for travel or trade.

As trade declined and the advantages of specialization disappeared for lack of markets, cities also declined, roads fell into disrepair, educational institutions declined or disappeared, and law and order broke down. It has been estimated that it was a thousand years after the collapse of the Roman Empire before the standard of living in Europe rose again to where it had been in Roman times. The presence or absence of effective government can be a major factor in economic development or retrogression.

Establishing law and order over a wide area not only enables producers to find large markets, and therefore take advantage of economies of scale in production, it also encourages people as well as products to move to where they are most in demand. When the British established control over areas of West Africa formerly controlled by different tribes and rulers, this enabled the Ibos from southern Nigeria to migrate to northern Nigeria in safety, setting up enterprises and pursuing careers in places where they would never have dared to locate before, among alien peoples. In various other parts of the world as well, during the period of European imperialism, vast numbers of immigrants from China, India, and Lebanon migrated to lands under the protection of imperial law, establishing many enterprises and creating whole industries that helped bring these societies into the modern world.

Another of the functions of government that affects economic development is its role in providing property rights—or failing to provide property rights. Many Third World countries suffer from the fact that, while property rights may exist, they are not realistically available to vast numbers of people. In some of these countries, a majority of the economic activity takes place "off the books" in the underground economy. For example, most of the housing in Egypt and Peru has been built illegally, whether because of numerous restrictions and red tape that impede building housing legally, or because of costly legal processes which poor people are unable to afford. In Egypt, where 4.7 million homes have been built illegally, legally registering a lot on state-owned desert land requires 77 bureaucratic procedures at 31 agencies—and these procedures can take five years or more. In Haiti, it can take 19 years to acquire property rights. In some countries, bribes are necessary to get officials to expedite legal processes, and often the poor are unable to offer a sufficient bribe.

In these circumstances, much of a country's total wealth may not be covered by property rights. In Peru, the value of real estate that is outside the legal system—that is, not covered by property rights—has been estimated to be more than a dozen times larger in value than all the foreign investment that has ever been put into the country throughout its entire history. Even in a desperately poor country like Haiti, the value of illegal urban real estate holdings has been estimated as four times the value of all the legally operating businesses in the country, nine times the value of all assets owned by the government and more than 150 times the value of all foreign investments in Haiti in its entire history. For the Third World as a whole and the former Communist countries as well, the estimated value of all the real estate that is not legally owned is more than 90 times the value of all the foreign aid to all Third World countries over a period of three decades.

What this means economically is that these vast, but legally unrecognized, assets cannot be used the way property is used in industrially advanced countries to promote further economic expansion. Many Americans have created their own businesses—some of which later grew into giant corporations—by borrowing money to get started, using their homes, farms, or other real estate as collateral to get the initial capital required.[2] But an Egyptian or a Peruvian or other Third World individual who wants to do the same thing cannot get a loan on a home that is not legally recognized as property, because banks and other financial institutions avoid lending money on assets whose ownership is unknown or unclear, and which therefore cannot be taken over in case of default. Lender's must think beyond stage one, not only to determine what their prospects of being repaid are, but also what their recourse will be if they are not repaid. By making property rights difficult to establish, a country's legal system has, in effect, frozen its own assets and thereby blocked its own economic development.

Real estate is just one of many economic assets lacking property rights in Third World countries. In many of these countries, unauthorized buses and taxis provide most of the public transportation, and unauthorized vendors supply most of the food sold in the markets and on the streets. According to the British magazine *The Economist*: "In a typical African country, barely one person in ten lives in a formal house"—that is, a house with property rights— "and only one person in ten holds a formal job." While these economic activities can go on without property rights, such assets cannot be used as building blocks for creating new corporations or venture capital, as they are in countries like the United States or the industrial nations of Western Europe. Legally, it is the same as if these assets did not exist—which in turn means that their potential use for further economic development is thwarted.

Those who do not think beyond stage one often think of property rights as simply benefits to those fortunate enough to own

---

[2] During its early struggling years, McDonald's was saved from financial ruin by real estate deals involving the land on which its franchised restaurants were located. But, without property rights on that land, McDonald's might well have disappeared into bankruptcy, long before it became an international corporate giant. See John F. Love, *McDonald's: Behind the Arches*, revised edition, pp. 152–155.

property. This ignores the role of property rights as a key link in a chain of events that enable people without property to generate wealth for themselves and the whole society.

One implication of this is that some Third World countries could gain the use of more capital by making property rights more accessible within their own borders than by a ten-fold increase in the amount of foreign aid they receive. Moreover, the increased capital would be in the hands of millions of ordinary people, while foreign aid goes into the hands of the political elite. In short, although property rights are often thought of as things that are important primarily to the affluent and the rich, these legal recognitions of existing assets may be especially needed by poor individuals in poor countries, if they do not wish to continue to be poor. Millions of Third World people have already demonstrated their ability to create, in the aggregate, vast amounts of wealth, even if their tangled legal systems have not yet demonstrated an ability to let that wealth readily become property that can be used for further expansion and development. As Peruvian economist Hernando de Soto concluded, after a worldwide study of this phenomenon:

> The lack of legal property thus explains why citizens in developing and former communist nations cannot make profitable contracts with strangers, cannot get credit, insurance, or utilities services. They have no property to lose. Because they have no property to lose, they are taken seriously as contracting partners only by their immediate family and neighbors. People with nothing to lose are trapped in the grubby basement of the precapitalist world.

Put differently, what property rights provide, in countries where these rights are readily accessible, is the ability of people to convert physical assets into financial assets, which in turn enables them to create additional wealth, whether individually or in combination with others. Property rights enable strangers to cooperate in economic ventures, some of which are beyond the means of any particular individual and must be undertaken by corporations which can mobilize the wealth of thousands or even millions of people, who cannot possibly all know each other. Moreover, property rights provide incentives to monitor their own economic activities more closely than government officials can—and protects them from the over-reaching caprices or corruption of such officials. In short, property rights are an integral part of a price-coordinated economy, without which that economy cannot function as efficiently. This in turn means that its people in general—not just property owners—cannot prosper as much as if it did operate more efficiently.

GEOGRAPHY

While the influence of the geographical settings in which peoples evolve has been widely recognized to one degree or another, the nature of that influence can vary greatly. It is relatively easy to understand the economic implications of the vast deposits of petroleum in the Middle East, the iron ore deposits of Western Europe, the tin in Malaysia, or the gold in South Africa. What may not be so obvious, but of equal or greater importance, is the crucial role of navigable waterways for transporting these and other natural resources, and the products resulting from them, to different regions of the Earth—creating wider cultural interactions in the process.

It is not simply that some people may be economically more fortunate because of the geographical setting in which they happen to live at a given time. More fundamentally, they themselves can become enduringly different people, partly as a result of their broader cultural contacts and the expanded universe of human experience on which they can draw. When British settlers first confronted the Iroquois on the east coast of North America in centuries past, there was a clash, not simply between the culture developed within the British isles versus the culture developed within the regions controlled by the Iroquois. There was a clash between cultural universes of very different sizes. The British were able to cross the Atlantic, in the first place, only by using trigonometry invented in Egypt, the compass invented in China, utilizing knowledge of astronomy developed in the Middle East, making calculations with numbers created in India, and drawing on other knowledge written in letters created by the Romans. Once ashore, the British had the advantage of weapons using gunpowder, which originated in Asia, and horses whose military uses had been developed in Central Asia and the Middle East.

Meanwhile, the Iroquois were geographically cut off from the civilizations of the Aztecs and the Incas, and had no way of knowing of their existence, much less drawing upon their economic, cultural, and military developments. Moreover, two vast oceans cut off the entire Western Hemisphere from developments in the rest of the world. The peoples of the Western Hemisphere were not as isolated as the people living in the Canary Islands or the Australian aborigines, since they had a certain amount of interaction among regions, but their range of cultural access was nowhere near as great as that of people living on the vast Eurasian land mass, where the majority of the human race has lived throughout recorded history.

Navigable Waterways

Access to the outside world is facilitated by navigable waterways—and access to these waterways is radically different in different part of the world. Although Africa is more than twice the size of Europe, its coastline is shorter than the European coastline. That is because the coastline of Europe twists and turns innumerable times, creating harbors where ships can anchor, protected from the rough waters of the open sea, while the African coastline is much smoother and has far fewer harbors. The enormous importance of rivers and harbors to economic and cultural development is indicated by the fact that nearly all the world's great cities developed on rivers or harbors, at least during the millennia before railroads and automobiles lowered the cost of land transport.

The fact that so many cities around the world arose on navigable waterways reflects in part vast differences in costs between transporting goods by water and transporting them by land. For example, in mid-nineteenth century America, before the transcontinental railroad was built, San Francisco could be reached both faster and cheaper from a port in China than it could be reached over land from the banks of the Missouri. In the city of Tiflis in the Caucasus, it was cheaper to import kerosene from Texas, across 8,000 miles of water, than to get it over land from Baku, less than 400 miles away. Similarly huge disparities between land transport and water transport costs have been common in Africa, in Japan, and in England before the railroad era. In the Ottoman Empire, the estimated cost of shipping wheat just 100 kilometers exceeded the value of the wheat itself.

Even after the development of roads and of motorized transport, trains, and planes, water transport has generally remained much cheaper than land transport. For example, transporting oil by ship costs about one-fourth of the cost of transporting it by pipeline, less than one-fifth of the cost of transporting it by railroad and little more than one percent of the cost of shipping it by truck.

The vast amounts of food and other products needed continuously to supply a city's population, and the vast amounts of raw material and finished merchandise to be moved in and out of a city to earn the money to pay for that population's consumption, have all been carried more cheaply by water. It is therefore hardly surprising that so many cities are on rivers—London on the Thames, Cairo on the Nile, Paris on the Seine, New York on the Hudson. Many other cities like Singapore, Sydney, and Stockholm are on harbors and still others are on huge lakes or inland seas like Chicago, Odessa, or Sevastopol. Nor should it be surprising that Western Europe, heavily criss-crossed by rivers, is one of the most densely urbanized regions of the world, while tropical Africa— where navigable waterways are much more scarce—has long remained one of the least urbanized areas in the world.

The relatively few cities that have arisen independently of waterways have usually had other transportation advantages. In the great desert regions, for example, the distances between sources of drinking water—compared to the distance that a camel can travel without water—determine which routes across the trackless sands or dry steppes are feasible and which are not. In turn, these routes and their traffic determine which of the oases have enough economic activity passing through them to become permanent settlements. Settlements at the crossroads of several routes through the desert—Samarkand in Central Asia, for example—could grow to be large cities, much as river and harbor ports grew into urban centers in other parts of the world. The development of railroads and, later, automobiles and trucks, brought a revolution in land transport that made water transport unnecessary to create major cities, which could now be based on railroad junctions (Atlanta[3]) or based on the automobile (Los Angeles).

The railroad revolution was particularly important in sub-Saharan Africa, which was largely lacking in both waterways and draft animals—the latter being victims of disease borne by the tsetse fly.

---

[3]An old Southern expression says: "Whether you are going to Heaven or Hell, you have to change in Atlanta."

Prior to the building of railroads by European colonial powers, Africans often carried freight on their heads. While this made for colorful caravans of porters, it was also a very expensive form of transport. In British West Africa, for example, it took 37 men to carry a ton of cocoa for a day's journey. A thousand times as much could be carried ten times as far by train, using half a dozen men.

Despite the importance of these modern developments, for most of history in most of the world, waterways have been crucial. During the European industrialization of the nineteenth century, every one of the early industrial regions had the benefit of navigable waterways. Where that advantage was lacking—as in parts of Eastern Europe and Mediterranean Europe, and especially in the Balkans, economic development lagged far behind that in such countries as Britain, France, and Germany. The standard of living in the less favored parts of Europe was much more like the standards of living in non-European countries than like those in the more advanced parts of the continent. The fossil fuels which were largely lacking in southern Europe, for example, often could not be brought into the interior by water—the only economically feasible way of delivering them.

Although urban growth was dramatic in much of nineteenth century Europe, few towns developed in the Balkans. As roads and railroads developed and were improved in the more developed parts of Europe, they remained virtually unknown in the Balkans, so that people living in Balkan villages were isolated from people in other villages less than 20 miles away. The Balkan mountains fractured the peninsula culturally as well as isolating it economically, thereby contributing to the tribalistic divisions and lethal hatreds which have long marked the region. Although the Balkans were rich in natural harbors, there were few rivers to connect these harbors to the hinterlands, which were often cut off by mountains. While much of nineteenth century Europe not only grew economically but became interconnected with other nations within

the continent and overseas, much of Eastern and Southeastern
Europe lived close to "self-sufficiency"—which is to say, it was isolated, poor, and backward.

   To have a large economic or cultural universe, it is not enough
that there be waterways. How *navigable* those waterways are is
crucial. Africa has the Nile and other great rivers, but these other
rivers have serious impediments to navigation, and have seldom
produced either cities or civilizations comparable to those of
Egypt. Because most of sub-Saharan Africa is more than a thousand feet above sea level, its rivers must come down from that alti-
tude on their way to the sea. The resulting rapids, cascades, and
waterfalls prevent even the greatest of sub-Saharan rivers from
providing access to and from the sea, in the way that the Hudson,
the Yangtze, the Danube, or other great commercial waterways of
the world can. Although Africa's Zaire River carries more water
than any of these three other rivers just mentioned, its waterfalls
alone are enough to preclude it from having the same significance
as an artery of trade or as a site for cities. Even African rivers that
are navigable may be navigable for some limited distances between
cascades or waterfalls, or by boats of limited size, or for some limited times during the rainy seasons. However, the dry season often
severely reduces or eliminates their navigability. There are no
mountain ranges in sub-Saharan Africa to catch snow, whose
melting would provide the water to sustain its waterways when
there is no rain, as mountain snows do in other parts of the world.

   Nor is Africa's geographic situation any better as regards harbors. Not only does the smooth African coastline provide few harbors, its coastal waters are often too shallow for large, ocean-going
ships to approach closely to the land. The net result was that, even
during centuries when much of the international trade of the
world went around Africa on its way between Europe and Asia,
relatively seldom did these ships attempt to stop and trade with

Africans. They could stop in those relatively few places where there were harbors or they could anchor offshore and have cargo loaded onto smaller craft that were able to make their way to land through the shallow coastal waters. Still, the higher costs of taking much longer to unload a given amount of cargo meant that there were severe constraints against international trade with even the coastal peoples of Africa, much less those in the vast interior hinterlands or at higher elevations. Moreover, the coastal plains of Africa average only 20 miles in width, often with steep escarpments behind them.

In short, with harbors as with rivers, Africa seldom had the geographic essentials for developing cities. Where cities or large-scale political units did develop in tropical Africa, it was typically where these geographical hindrances were not as great.

Disparities between the costs of land transport and water transport translate into similar disparities in the reach of trade and in the range of goods which are feasible to trade by nations and peoples with and without navigable waterways. Huge transportation costs shrink the economic universe, severely limiting how far given goods can be carried, and severely limiting which goods have sufficient value condensed into a small size and weight (gold or diamonds, for example) to be feasible to transport over land for substantial distances. These same high transportation costs shrink the cultural universe as well, handicapping not only economic development but, more importantly, the development of the people themselves, who lack access to as wide a range of other people's knowledge, skills, and technologies as do people who are situated in port cities and other cultural crossroads.

The significance of particular geographic features—mountains, rivers, climate, soil, etc.—is even greater when these features are viewed in combination. For example, the effect of rainfall on agriculture depends not only on how much rainfall there is but also on the ability of the soil to hold it. Thus a modest amount of rainfall may be sufficient for a flourishing agriculture on the absorbent loess soils of northern China, while rain falling on the limestone soils of the Balkans may drain off rapidly underground. Similarly, the economic value of navigable waterways depends on the lands adjacent to them. Navigable rivers which go through land without the resources for either industry or agriculture—the Amazon for example—are of little economic value,[4] even though navigable waterways in general have been crucial to the economic and cultural development of other regions more fully endowed with other resources.

In Russia as well, waterways isolated from the major natural resources of the country, as well as from each other, cannot match the economic role of rivers which flow into one another and then into the sea, after passing through agriculturally or industrially productive regions, as in Western Europe. The Volga is Russia's premier river for shipping, even though there are other Russian rivers which have more than twice as much water flow, because the Volga passes through areas containing most of the resources and people of the country. Larger rivers in Siberia, which drain northward into the Arctic Ocean—when they are not frozen and cannot flow at all— have no such economic significance as the Volga.

Similarly, harbors that are not as deep, not as wide, nor as well-sheltered as other harbors, may nevertheless become busy ports if they represent the only outlets for productive regions in the vicinity, as has been the case of Genoa in northwestern Italy or Mombasa in East Africa. Similarly, the port of Dubrovnik on the Dalmatian coast, strategically located for the international trade

---

[4] The Amazon, for example, is by far the world's greatest river but the soils in its region have been characterized as "startlingly poor" and it has led to no great cities being established along its banks. See Jonathan B. Tourtellot, "The Amazon: Sailing a Jungle Sea," *Great Rivers of the World*, edited by Margaret Sedeen (Washington: National Geographic Society, 1984), p. 302.

routes of the Middle Ages, flourished despite a harbor that was not particularly impressive in itself. While the historic role of London as a world port has depended on the Thames, this river is also not especially impressive in itself, but has simply provided an outlet for impressive industrial and commercial facilities nearby.

Sometimes a variety of favorable geographical features exist in combination within a given region, as in northwestern Europe, and sometimes virtually all are lacking, as in much of tropical Africa, while still other parts of the world have some of these favorable features but not others. The consequences include not only large variations in economic wellbeing but, more fundamentally, large variations in the skills and experience—the human capital—of the people themselves. Given the enormous range of combinations of geographical features, the peoples from different regions of the earth have had highly disparate opportunities to develop particular skills and economic experience or to acquire them from others. International migrations then put these peoples with disparate skills, aptitudes, and outlooks in proximity to one another and in competition with one another in other lands, often producing very different economic and social outcomes.

Among the more geographically fortunate parts of the world, in terms of having the natural resources needed for the development of a modern industrial economy, as well as the navigable waterways to carry both these resources and the products resulting from them, have been Northern and Western Europe. Iron ore and coal deposits, the key ingredients of steel manufacturing and the heavy industry dependent on it, are concentrated in the Ruhr valley, in Wales, in Sweden, and in the region so bitterly fought over by France and Germany, Alsace-Lorraine. In addition to the broad coastal plains which have provided the peoples of Western Europe with much prime agricultural land and with navigable rivers, Europe in general has many peninsulas, islands, and numerous harbors that give the continent excellent access to the sea.

Climate

Favorable climate is also a factor. The Western European climate is greatly benefitted by the flow of the Gulf stream, as a separate waterway cutting through the North Atlantic, just as other streams flow through land. This stream of warm water, originating in the Gulf of Mexico, warms Western Europe to give it milder winters than places at similar latitudes in the Western Hemisphere or in Asia. London, for example, is farther north than any place in the 48 contiguous United States, yet it has milder winters than New York City, much less cities in Minnesota or Wisconsin.

Eastern, Central, and Mediterranean Europe do not share all these advantages. The Gulf Stream's influence on the climate of European nations on the Atlantic coast becomes progressively less in the more distant central and eastern portions of the continent, where rivers are frozen for more days of the year and where winters are longer and more bitterly cold. The natural resources required for modern industry are also less abundant and, in many places, virtually non-existent in Central and Eastern Europe. The broad coastal plains of Northern Europe have no counterparts in the Balkans, where hills and mountains come down close to the sea and the coastal harbors often have no navigable rivers to link them to the hinterlands. Spain has likewise been lacking in navigable rivers and Sicily lacking in both rivers and rainfall.

These sharp differences in geographical advantages have been reflected not only in great disparities in wealth among the different regions of Europe, but also in similarly large differences in skills, industrial experience, and whole ways of life among the peoples of these regions. Thus, when the peoples of the Mediterranean migrated to the United States or to Australia, for example, they did not bring with them the industrial skills or the whole modern way of life found among German or English immigrants. What they did bring with them was a frugality born of centuries of struggle for survival in the less productive lands and waters of the Mediterranean, and a power of endurance and persistence born of the same circumstances. The ability of Italian immigrants to endure poor and cramped living conditions and to save out of very low wages, which caused comment among those around them, whether in other European countries or in the Western Hemisphere or Australia, had both geographical and historical roots. Similar characteristics have marked various other Mediterranean peoples, but the Italians are a particularly revealing example because they include not only the Mediterranean people of the south but also people from the industrial world of the Po River valley in the north, whose geographical, economic, and cultural characteristics are much more similar to those found among Northern and Western Europeans. Northern and southern Italians have long differed economically and socially, not only in Italy, but also in Australia, the United States, and Argentina.

The enduring consequences of the different skills and experiences possessed by people from different parts of Europe can be seen in the fact that the average income of immigrants from Southern and Eastern Europe to the United States in the early twentieth century was equal to what was earned by the bottom 15 percent among immigrants from England, Scotland, Holland, or Norway. Illiteracy was higher among immigrants from Southern and Eastern Europe. In school, their children tended to lag behind the children of either native-born Americans or the children of immigrants from Northern and Western Europe, while their I.Q. scores were often very similar to those of American blacks, and were sometimes lower.

Nor was all this peculiar to American society. In pre-World War II Australia, immigrants from southern Italy, Dalmatia, Macedonia, and the Greek countryside were typically illiterate and spoke primarily their local dialects, rather than the official languages of their respective home countries. More than three quarters of these Southern European immigrants to Australia were from the rugged hills or mountains, the steep coastlines or islands of the region, rather than from the urban areas or plains. Although these remote areas were eventually drawn into the modern world, the skills of their peoples continued to lag behind the skills of peoples in other parts of Europe that were more industrially advanced and this was reflected in their earnings in Australia, as in the United States. As late as the 1970s, the median earnings of immigrants to Australia from Greece, Italy, or Yugoslavia fell below the earnings of immigrants from West Germany or from English-speaking countries. Southern Europeans in Australia remained under-represented in professional and technical occupations, and from nearly half among the Italian immigrants to an absolute majority among the Greek and Yugoslavian immigrants were unskilled laborers. These patterns were not simply a result of such subjective factors as others' stereotypes, perceptions, or racism, but in fact reflected historical realities, however much additional penumbra of prejudice may have developed around those realities, or remained resistant to change after the realities themselves began to change with the assimilation and rising skill levels of the newcomers.

In addition to the effect of climate on the flow of water—freezing rivers in Russia during the winter and the drying up of rivers in tropical Africa after the rainy season is over—it has long had a major direct effect on agriculture. Moreover, agriculture has been the place where the vast majority of the peoples of the world have worked throughout almost all of history. Even countries that are heavily industrial and commercial today were primarily agricultural until recent centuries. In the United States, for example, it was 1920 before more than half the American population lived in cities.

Temperature and rainfall determine what crops can be grown where. In extreme cases, they determine that no crops at all can be grown, as in deserts and in places where the land is frozen year around, such as in parts of Siberia. In places where moisture-laden air blows across a mountain range, it is not uncommon for the rainfall on the side where the moisture originates to be several times as great as in the "rain shadow" on the other side of the mountains, where the air goes after it has lost most of its moisture while rising over the crests. On some western slopes of southern Italy's Apennines Mountains, for example, the annual rainfall reaches 2,000 millimeters while parts of the eastern slopes get as little as 300–500 millimeters. Similarly, in the American Pacific Northwest, precipitation on parts of the west side of the Cascade Mountains averages up to ten times as much as on parts of the Columbia Plateau to the east. Obviously the agricultural possibilities presented to the people living on one side of the mountain range differ greatly from those presented to people living on the other side. They must grow different crops and acquire different skills and experiences while doing so.

Climate also affects the diffusion of knowledge and experience. Because climate tends to vary less from east to west than it does from north to south, knowledge of particular crops and animals that flourish in a particular climate likewise spread more readily from east to west than from north to south. Thus the cultivation of rice spread from China all the way across the Eurasian land mass into Europe, while the cultivation of bananas could not spread from Central America into Canada, even though that is a shorter distance, because the climate differs so much between Central America and Canada. The same goes for the domestication or hunting of animals peculiar to a particular climate. The knowledge of such things likewise spreads more readily from east to west, than it did from north to south. Nor could knowledge of the crops, flora and fauna in the temperate zone of South America diffuse smoothly to the temperate zone of North America, because many of the techniques and practices could not spread through the vast tropical regions between these two temperate zones. Very different plants and animals existed in the tropics, so that much of the knowledge and many of the techniques from the temperate zones could not be applied in the tropics, and therefore could not be transmitted through the tropics to temperate zones on the other side.

Temperature is, of course, not the only aspect of climate. Rainfall is another. Knowledge and techniques of agriculture that apply in a wet climate may not all be usable in arid regions. Therefore differences in rainfall patterns can produce cultural isolation as regards agricultural techniques, just as natural barriers like mountains or deserts can produce cultural isolation in general. Those isolated climatically have likewise been unable to draw upon the knowledge and experience of peoples in similar climates elsewhere, when there have been hundred or thousands of miles of very different climate patterns in between.

During the many centuries when ships were moved on the seas by the power of the wind in their sails, knowledge of particular wind patterns and ocean currents in particular regions of the world was crucial to the ability to carry on trade among different societies. Much of this knowledge was as localized as knowledge of the plants and animals peculiar to particular geographic settings. Knowledge of sailing in general was not enough when trying to sail off the west coast of Africa, for example, in places where it was easy for Europeans to use the wind and currents in that region to get in but hard to use them to get back out again. Conversely, sailors familiar with the monsoon winds of Asia could sail westward as far as Africa during the times of the year when those winds were blowing in that direction, and then return home later, after the time came for the winds to shift direction and begin blowing eastward.

Like other special knowledge of local or regional conditions, knowledge of wind patterns and ocean currents, and the techniques developed to deal with these localized patterns, tended to be confined to those living in the area. Put differently, various regions tended to develop different knowledge and techniques. Thus, for example, those countries which became leading seafaring nations and naval powers in the Mediterranean during the Middle Ages were not able to play the same role in the later era of trade and warfare in the Atlantic, where the waters were much rougher, and the wind and weather conditions more severe. Those nations which had been the leading naval powers in Europe in the earlier era, when the Mediterranean was the principal avenue of waterborne commerce and naval warfare, were unable to match the upstart Atlantic naval powers when the central theater of trade and warfare shifted to the Atlantic after the Europeans discovered the Western Hemisphere.

POPULATION

Some of the worst poverty in the world today can be found in thinly-populated regions like sub-Saharan Africa. Meanwhile, population density is several times higher in much more prosperous Japan. There are also densely populated poor countries, such as Bangladesh, but there are even more densely populated places like Switzerland and Singapore, with far higher standards of living. The United States and Tanzania have very similar population densities, but radically different economic levels. Clearly, there are other factors that have much more to do with prosperity than population does. Indeed, a case can be made for many regions of the world that it is precisely the thinly spread population which makes it so expensive to provide electricity, sewage lines, and medical care that many of these people are often without such things.

In some ultimate sense, there must of course be a limit to the earth's capacity to sustain human life. But there are ultimate limits to many things—perhaps all things—and yet that provides little or no practical guidance as to how close we are to those limits or what the consequences are of various alternatives today. There are ultimate limits to how fast a given automobile will go, and yet we may drive it for years without ever reaching even half of that ultimate speed, because there are much narrower limits to how fast we can drive safely through city streets or even on highways. As a young man, John Stuart Mill brooded over the fact that there was an ultimate limit to the amount of music that could be produced by using the eight notes of the musical scale. But, at that time, Brahms and Tchaikovsky had not yet been born nor jazz yet conceived, and rock music was more than a century away. Ultimate limits alone tell us virtually nothing useful about whether there is or is not a practical problem.

If we were in fact approaching those ultimate limits, whether in food supply, natural resources, or other necessities of life, their rising prices would not only inform us, but force us to change course, without public exhortations or politically-imposed limitations. Indeed, many political solutions are as inconsistent as they are counterproductive. For example, there are restrictions on the use of water by the general public, imposed by the same political authorities who supply water below cost to farmers. These farmers consequently grow crops requiring huge amounts of water from costly government irrigation projects in the California desert, instead of leaving such crops to be grown in the rainy regions of the world, where ample water is supplied free from the clouds. Although the water is costly to the government—which is to say, the taxpayers—it is cheap to the farmers, and is used as if it were abundant.

Food shortages and famines have sometimes been used as evidence that population has outgrown the food supply. But hunger and starvation in modern times have almost always reflected local problems such as crop failures in a given area, combined with difficulties in getting enough food into the stricken region fast enough to prevent death from either malnutrition or diseases to which the people have been made vulnerable by malnutrition.

In some very poor countries, the roads and other infrastructure are not sufficiently developed to carry vast amounts of food to widely scattered people with the urgency that is needed. All too often, in both poor and more affluent countries, the famines have resulted from human error or malice or military operations that disrupt food distribution systems. During the First World War, for example, the Allied naval blockade prevented food from reaching many in central Europe:

> Germans were forced to eat their dogs and cats (the latter came to be known as "roof rabbits") as well as bread made from potato peels and sawdust. Civilian deaths by starvation climbed to hundreds of thousands per year.

None of this had anything to do with overpopulation. Neither did the man-made famine in the Ukraine in the 1930s, which took millions of lives, and which Josef Stalin used to break the back of resistance to his regime.

"Overpopulation" theories do not stand up well to empirical scrutiny. But they do not have to. They have in fact remained popular for more than two centuries, in the face of large and growing evidence of their falsity. Even within Malthus' own life-time, his prediction that growing numbers of people tended to cause their standard of living to be reduced was falsified by empirical evidence of rising population and rising living standards occurring simultaneously. That has continued to be the general pattern ever since. Wars, natural disasters, and other local disruptions of food supplies have caused famines from time to time in various places around the world, though less so than in centuries past, when the world's population was a fraction of what it is today. Indeed, obesity and a search for export markets for agricultural surpluses are problems for a growing number of countries today.

Even in a poverty-stricken country like India, the number of people has been nowhere close to what the land could support. A twentieth century study found:

> Half the population of India lives on less than a quarter of the total available land, and one-sixth is concentrated on less than 6 percent of the land. At the other extreme, vast areas continue to be almost uninhabited.

Photographs of crowded cities in Third World countries may create the impression that there is not enough room for the populations of these countries and that this somehow accounts for their poverty. However, crowding is what cities are all about, whether in poor countries or in rich countries. Park Avenue has more people per square mile than in many Third World villages or urban slums. Crowding lowers the cost per person of supplying everything from electricity to running water to sewage lines, movie theaters and ambulance services. That is why there have been crowded cities in countries with vast amounts of open space, whether in twentieth century India or nineteenth century America.

IMPLICATIONS

All the numerous and interacting factors behind economic development make it virtually impossible that different parts of the world would all have equal development, and therefore equal standards of living, at any given time. Yet the puzzlement, unease and dissatisfaction caused by seeing large economic disparities between societies have created demands for explanations—usually without creating an equal demand for years of study of the historical, geographic, and economic factors behind these disparities. Instead, there has been a demand for simple and emotionally satisfying explanations, especially melodramatic explanations with ideological overtones, such as "exploitation" theories. "Overpopulation" is also a simple explanation that lends itself to melodrama and to solutions favored by those inclined toward controlling other people's lives.

Exploitation theories explain the wealth of some by the poverty of others, whether comparing nations or classes within nations. Sadly, however, many of the those who are said to be exploited have had very little to exploit and many of those described as "dispossessed" have never possessed very much in the first place. Moreover, the actual behavior of those described as exploiters often shows them shunning those that they are said to exploit, in favor of dealing with more prosperous people, from whom they expect to earn more money. Thus, most American international trade and investment goes to high-income nations like those in Western Europe or the more prosperous regions of Asia, such as Japan or Singapore, with only a minute fraction of that trade or investment going to Africa or to the more poverty stricken regions of Asia or the Middle East. Conversely, the United States is itself the largest recipient of investments by foreigners. Similarly, within the United States, capitalists are far more anxious to establish businesses in middle class or wealthy communities, rather than businesses in blighted ghettos or on poverty-stricken Indian reservations.

At particular times and places in history, conquerors have indeed extracted wealth from the conquered peoples, but the real question is: How much of today's economic differences between nations and peoples does that explain? Spain, for example, extracted vast amounts of gold and silver from its conquered lands and peoples in the Western Hemisphere, at great economic and human costs to those who were subjugated. But much of this wealth was quickly spent, buying imported goods from other countries, rather than developing Spain itself, which has remained one of the poorer nations in Western Europe. Meanwhile, Germany—lacking colonies of any serious economic consequence for the German economy, for most of its history—became one of the most prosperous nations in Europe. Switzerland and the Scandinavian countries have had no colonies at all and yet have been among the most prosperous countries in Europe and the world.

In Asia, Japan embarked on an ambitious campaign of conquest in the twentieth century and its behavior toward its conquered fellow Asians was as brutal and ruthless as that of Spain toward those whom it had subjugated in the Western Hemisphere. Moreover, Japan used its own lack of natural resources as a justification for its actions. Yet, after Japan's defeat in World War II led to the loss of all its colonies and conquered lands, the Japanese economy not only recovered from the devastations of war, it rose to new heights. The natural resources that it lacked could be bought in international markets for less than the cost of conquering other countries and maintaining armies there to keep them subjugated.

Exploitation theories are sometimes based on assumptions of ignorance and naivete on the part of some groups, such as Third World peoples, as well as wily and unscrupulous outsiders who are able to make high profits from paying the indigenous people less than their goods are really worth in the world market. Obviously, everyone is ignorant of things they have not encountered before and those living in isolated parts of the world place whatever value they do on new products, based in part on their novelty. But the question is: How long can such a situation last? More specifically, can it last long enough to explain international differences in income and wealth? An observer writing about West Africa, early in the twentieth century, reported that the ability of foreign traders to obtain much gold and ivory in that region for a little inexpensive colored cloth and cheap knives had already been ended by the growth of competition, and that consequently "the margin of profit was diminished." This is what anyone should have expected on the basis of elementary economic principles. Dated anecdotes from the earlier period might continue to be repeated for many years afterward, but the only current exploitation they demonstrate is exploitation of the gullibility of those who are led to believe that this represents a serious explanation of international economic differences.

No given factor can account for the large disparities in economic development among the countries of the world. Nor is the relative influence of any particular factor likely to remain the same over time. Although various geographic factors have played a major role in the economic opportunities available to various peoples, economic development also affects the influence of geography. The invention of railroads and trucks has made available low-cost transport for the first time in regions lacking in navigable waterways and draft animals, such as much of West Africa. Production and sales of cocoa, cotton, and tin began to flourish on a large scale in that part of the world after railroads replaced the costly use of human porters, who were very limited in the size of the loads they could carry. Even mountains became less formidable barriers after techniques of tunneling and blasting through them developed, while airplanes have flown over these mountains and shrunk the role of distance in general. Radios and telephones made long-distance communications possible for the first time in many poor and isolated areas, and the Internet has put the peoples of the whole world in instant communication with one another. In short, economic development has reduced the role of geographic factors, which had made economic development possible in the first place.

SOURCES

CHAPTER 1: POLITICS VERSUS ECONOMICS

Data on spending and taxing in New York City are from an article on pages 27 to 35 of the Winter 2003 issue of *City Journal*, titled "Bloomberg to City: Drop Dead," by Steven Malanga. The effects of subsidized rice in India are discussed on page 313 of *India Unbound* by Gurcharand Das. The effect of subsidized train fares in India is from page 8 of a special section on India in *The Economist* of June 2, 2001 under the title, "The Rich Get Richer." The statement about the Indian government's tardiness in responding to a cyclone is quoted from page 535 of Indian economist Barun S. Mitra's article, "Dealing with Natural Disaster: Role of the Market," in the December 2000 issue of *Journal des Economistes et des Etudes Humaines*. The information on the effects of California's price controls on electricity supply is from page 10 of "California's Electricity Crisis," by Jerry Taylor and Peter Van Doren, *Policy Analysis* paper number 406 of the Cato Institute. Gunnar Myrdal's thumbnail sketch of central planning is from page 131 of his book, *Asian Drama*, abridged edition published in 1972 by Vintage Press. The use of food and electricity in an Israeli kibbutz, before and after prices were charged for them, is discussed on pages 332 and 333 of *Heaven on Earth: the Rise and Fall of Socialism* by Joshua Muracchik, published in 2002 by Encounter Books. The excessive use of resources by the Soviet Union is from pages 128 to 137 of a book by two Soviet economists: *The Turning Point: Revitalizing the Soviet Economy* by Nikolai Shmelev and Vladimir Popov, published in 1989 by Doubleday. The statement about a Soviet queue for men's undershirts is from page 169 of *An Old Wife's Tale* by Midge Decter. Data on the Gross National Income per capita in China and in India are from two publications of the World Bank—*World Tables 1992* and *World Development Indicators*, both published by Johns Hopkins University Press. The data from 1970 to 1991 are from the former (Table 2) and for 2000 are from the latter (Table 1.1). India's relaxation of government controls over its economy was reported in the distinguished British magazine, *The Economist*, June 2, 2001, page 13. The bird droppings found on bread in the Soviet Union and its subsequent re-baking into new bread was reported on pages 163 and 164 of *The Age of Delirium: The Decline and Fall of the Soviet Union* by David Satter, published by Yale University Press in 1996. The quotation from Congressman Kucinich is from page A29 of the March 14, 2003 issue of the *San Francisco Chronicle* in an op-ed essay titled "Water is a Matter of Public Debate" by Dennis Kucinich. The quotations from the Soviet Economists are from page 61 of *The Turning Point: Revitalizing the Soviet Economy* by Nikolai Shmelev and Vladimir Popov.

CHAPTER 2: FREE AND UNFREE LABOR

Information on debt peonage in India is from an article titled "The Social Psychology of Modern Slavery," in the April 9, 2000 issue of *Scientific American*, April 9, 2002. The experiences of Paul Williams are from *Paul R. Williams, Architect: A Legacy of Style* by Karen E. Hudson, published in 1993 by Rizzoli International Publications. The experiences of F. W. Woolworth are from *Remembering Woolworth* by Karen Plunkett-Powell, especially on pages 19, 20, 30 and 49. Information on the early work habits of the richest Americans is from page 14 of *A Portrait of the Affluent in America Today* (New York: U. S. Trust, 1998). Information on the 400 richest Americans is from pages 80 and 81 of the September 30, 2002 issue of *Forbes* magazine, in an article by William P. Barrett titled "The March of the 400." Rags-to-riches stories from India can be found in *India Unbound* by Gurcharand Das, on pages 187–195, 207–210, 246–248. The quotation from Professor Peter Bauer about social mobility in Britain is from page 127 of his book, *From Subsistence to Exchange*, published in 2000 by the Princeton University Press. Data on labor productivity in India and the United States are from page 65 of the September 8, 2001 issue of *The Economist*, under the title "Unproductive." The relative productivity of British companies run by British and American managements was reported on page 52 of the October 12, 2002 issue of *The Economist* in an article titled, "Blame the Bosses." The quotation about not being able to make a man worth more by making it illegal for anyone to offer him less is from page 237 of *The Wisdom of Henry Hazlitt*, published in 1993 by the Foundation for Economic Education, 1993. Job security laws in Germany and their consequences were reported in the July 14, 2001 issue of *The Economist* on page 47, under the title "No Great Harm, No Good Either." Job guarantees to engineers in India are mentioned on page 46 of "Impossible India's Improbable Chance," by David Gardner in *The World in 2001*, published by the British magazine, *The Economist*. The information on Poland's job security agreements is from *The Economist* of March 23, 2002, pages 58 and 59. The case of the Indian fertilizer plant which continued to employ workers, even though they were producing no fertilizer, is from pages 160 of *India Unbound* by Gurcharand Das. The low percentage of the country's industrial output produced by government-owned enterprises is from page 161 of the same book. The comparisons of British and American burglary rates is from page 165 of *Guns and Violence* by Joyce Lee Malcolm. The data on burglaries in occupied and unoccupied homes in the United States, Britain, Canada, and the Netherlands is from page 140 of *Point Blank: Guns and Violence in America* by Gary Kleck and the dramatic decline in burglaries in Kennesaw, Georgia, after each household was required to have a firearm is reported on page 136. Data on the sharp rise in murder rates after the legal reforms of the 1960s is from page 409 of *Crime and Human Nature* by James Q. Wilson and Richard J. Herrnstein. Data on the increased risk of becoming a victim of a violent crime is from page 4 of *Criminal Violence, Criminal Justice* by Charles H. Silberman. Data and graphs showing crime rates and incarceration rates in Britain, Australia, New Zealand, and the United States are from an article titled "Does Prison Work?" in the Summer 2002–2003 issue of the Australian publication *Policy*, published by the Centre for Independent Studies in St. Leonards, New South Wales. The history of firearms laws and murder rates in London and New York are from pages 141–144, 223 and 225 of *Guns and Violence* by Joyce Lee Malcolm.

The episode involving taking a shopper in custody to be forced to serve as a juror is from a front-page story in the August 20, 2002 issue of the

Wall Street Journal, under the title, "When the Jury Box Runs Low, Deputies Hit the Wal-Mart." The use of Irish immigrants, instead of slaves, for hazardous work is mentioned in the Modern Library edition of *The Cotton Kingdom* by Frederick Law Olmstead on pages 70 and 215; on pages 186–187 of *Life and Labor in the Old South* by U. B. Phillips; on page 394 of *The Americans* (1969 edition) by J. C. Furnas; on page 101 of the second volume of *The Americans* by Daniel Boorstin; pages 301–302 of *American Negro Slavery*, by U. B. Phillips; and page 520 of the second volume of *History of Agriculture in the Southern United States* by Lewis C. Gray. The various roles played by slaves in countries around the world and a capsule history of slavery around the world can be found in Chapter 7 of my book *Race and Culture*. The use of slaves as human sacrifices was discussed on page 26 of *Human Bondage in Southeast Asia* by Bruno Lasker, published in 1950 by the University of North Carolina Press; on page 191 of *Slavery and Social Death: A Comparative Study* by Orlando Patterson, published in 1982 by the Harvard University Press; and on page 325 of *Indians of North America*, second edition, by Harold E. Driver published by the University of Chicago Press in 1975. The better treatment accorded slaves in occupations requiring individual initiative, such as divers in the Carolina swamps or in tobacco processing, was described on pages 114–116, 119–120 of Olmsted's *Cotton Kingdom* on page 188 of *Slavery in the Americas* (1961) by Herbert S. Klein and on page 127 of *A Journey in the Seabord Slave States* (1969) by Frederick Law Olmsted. The case of the slave who was a river boat captain over a crew that included both black and white sailors is from the December 1962 issue of the *Mississippi Valley Historical Review*, pages 472–484, under the title, "Simon Gray, Riverman: A Slave Who Was Almost Free." Frederick Douglass' comment on urban slaves was quoted from page 110 of *Slavery in the Cities* by Richard C. Wade. Information on the economics of the Soviet gulags is from Chapter 2 of *Labor Camp Socialism: The Gulag in the Soviet Totalitarian System* by Galina M. Ivanova, a scholar in the Russian Academy of Sciences in Moscow, in an English translation published in London by M.E. Sharpe. The superfluous railroads built at the cost of gulag prisoners' lives were mentioned on pages 123 to 124 of *Behind the Facade of Stalin's Command Economy*, edited by Paul R. Gregory and published in 2001 by the Hoover Institution Press. Books on white inden- tured servants in colonial America include *White Servitude in Colonial America: An Economic Analysis* by David Galenson and *Colonists in Bondage* by Abbott Emerson Smith. The estimate that more than half of the white population outside of New England arrived in colonial America as inden- tured servants is from pages 3–4 of the latter. The history of coerced Chi- nese indentured labor shipped from the port of Macao in the nineteenth century is discussed on pages 74, 98, 124, and 128 of *Chinese Bondage in Peru* by Watt Stewart and pages 18–19, 27–29, 80, and 117 of *A Study of the Chinese in Cuba* by Duvon Clough Corbitt. The unscrupulous methods used to gather indentured labor in Britain to be shipped to its Western Hemisphere colonies are discussed in Chapter 4 of *Colonists in Bondage* by Abbott Emerson Smith. The purchase of freedom in ancient times was mentioned on pages 18–19, 25, and 83 of *The Slave Systems of Greek and Roman Antiquity* by William L. Westermann. Purchase of freedom later in the Western Hemisphere is mentioned on pages 7–8, 24–26, 31–34, 63, 86, 88, 90, 91, 96, 125, 225–226 of *Neither Slave Nor Free: The Freedmen of African Descent in the Slave Societies of the New World*, edited by David W. Cohen and Jack P. Greene. Lincoln's remark about every drop of blood drawn with the lash being repaid in blood drawn by the sword is from his second inaugural address.

CHAPTER 3: THE ECONOMICS OF MEDICAL CARE

Information on the Soviet Union's medical care system is from a front-page story in the *Wall Street Journal* of August 18, 1987, titled "Soviet Health System, Despite Early Claims, Is Riddled by Failures." Japan's shorter and more numerous patient visits to doctor's offices, compared to such visits in the United States, are reported on page 350 of *American Health Care* results on page 352, edited by Roger D. Feldman. Similar experiences in Korea and in Canada's Quebec province is from page 352 of the same book. Canada's medical system's problems were discussed in *Business Week* magazine, August 31, 1998 in a story titled "Canada's Health-Care System Isn't a Model Any- more," beginning on page 36. Information on Britain's government-run medical system is from page 76 of an essay titled "Will Money Cure the NHS?" by Paul Wallace in *The World in 2003*, published by *The Economist*. The quoted material about France's health-care system is from an article titled "A Hypochondriac's Paradise" in the British magazine, *New Statesman*, September 18, 1998, page 28. London's newspaper *The Guardian* reported the story of the British girl who received a breast implant in its November 9, 1998 issue, page 6, under the title, "Girl, 12, to Get Breast Implant." The San Francisco cardiologist who ordered unneeded bypass surgery is mentioned in a front page story in the *San Francisco Chronicle* of November 2, 2002 under the headline: "Doctors Raised Red Flags in 1997." China's medical problems were reported in *The Economist* of November 7, 1998 on page 71, in an article titled "Pharmaceuticals in China: Overdosed" and in *The China Business Review* of November 1, 1998, in an article titled "Medical Investment Alternatives," beginning on page 47. The 10,000 people in Britain who had waited 15 months or more for surgery were reported in *The Economist* magazine of London on page 55 of its April 13, 2002 issue. The British woman whose cancer surgery was postponed until it had to be cancelled because the cancer had become inoperable during the long delays was mentioned in *The Economist* of November 24, 2001, on page 52. Bribes in Tokyo hospitals are mentioned on page 351 of *American Health Care*. China's medical problems were reported in *The Economist* of November 7, 1998 on page 71, in an article titled "Pharmaceuticals in China: Overdosed" and in *The China Business Review* of November 1, 1998, in an article titled "Medical Investment Alternatives," beginning on page 47. The story about the woman who bought several pairs of eyeglasses with her medical savings account is from page D1 of the November 2, 2002 issue of the *Wall Street Journal* in a story "Getting Uncle Sam to Cover Your Massage: Rush to Use Up Medical Savings Accounts Prompts Creative Reading of Rules." The proportion of uninsured people in various age brackets is from the front page of the *Wall Street Journal* of March 17, 2003, under the title, "A Young Woman, An Appendectomy, and a $19,000 Debt" by Lucette Lagnado. The problems created by high jury awards and the resulting rise in the cost of medical malpractice insurance are discussed in the February 27, 2003 issue of the *Wall Street Journal OnLine* in an article titled "Delivering Justice" by

Walter Olson and in a front-page article in the print edition of the same newspaper on June 24, 2002, titled "Assigning Liability," beginning on page A4. The quotation from the medical study of the causes of infant brain damage and cerebral palsy was from page A12 of the February 27, 2003 issue of the *Wall Street Journal*, under the title "Delivering Justice" by Walter Olson. The quotation from the official of Pfizer is from page 68 of the January 20, 2003 issue of *Fortune* magazine, under the title "The $10 Billion Pill" which began on page 58. The fact that the development of a new drug costs hundreds of millions of dollars has been reported in many places, including the multi-tiered pricing at such places as the UCLA Medical Center, is covered in a front-page article in the *Wall Street Journal* of March 17, 2004 titled "A Young Woman, An Appendectomy, and a $19,000 debt" by Lucette Lagnado. The same article is the source of data on the ages of uninsured Americans. The fact that developing a new medication costs hundreds of millions of dollars has been reported in a number of places, including page A15 of the November 11, 2001 issue of *The New Yorker* under the title "No Profit, No Cure," by James Surowiecki in the July 22, 2002 issue of the *Wall Street Journal* in an editorial titled "Drug Prices: A Much-Needed Primer." The Food and Drug Administration's ban on advertising the uses of aspirin as a heart-attack preventative is discussed on pages 285–286 of *American Health Care*, edited by Roger D. Feldman, in an article titled "Ignorance is Death: The FDA's Advertising Restrictions," by Paul Rubin. The fact that some clinical trials of new drugs add an additional eight years to the approval process is reported on pages 6 and 7 of the February 2003 issue of *Fraser Forum* under the title "Using Our Heads on Head-to-Head Trials," by John H. Graham. The pharmaceutical drug testing that takes eight years is discussed on pages 6 and 7 of the February 2003 issue of *Fraser Forum* in an article titled, "Using Our Heads on Head-to-Head Trials," by John H. Graham Fraser.

CHAPTER 4: THE ECONOMICS OF HOUSING

The affordability of a two-bedroom apartment on a nurse's salary in various cities was reported on page 34 of the December 7, 2002 issue of *The Econo-*

mist under the title "The Roof That Costs Too Much." The increase in the number of commuters into the San Francisco Bay area from outlying counties was reported in the March 6, 2003 issue of the *San Francisco Chronicle* on page A15 under the title "Census Sees Long Ride to Work" by Michael Cabanatuan. The nearly four-fold rise of home prices in Palo Alto during the 1970s, the closing of several schools there as enrollments declined, and a decline in the city's population in general, were mentioned on pages 10, 85, 89, and 90 of a 1982 study by the Stanford Environmental Law Society titled *Land Use and Housing on the San Francisco Peninsula*, edited by Thomas M. Hagler. The use of political power by affluent northern Californians to protect the status quo in their communities is covered in many parts of this same study. Statistics on the decline of the black population in various California communities between the 1990 and 2000 censuses are from the following publications of the U.S. Bureau of the Census: *1990 Census of Population: General Population Characteristics California* PC–1–6 Section 1 of 3; *2000 Profiles of General Demographic Characteristics California*; *2000 Profiles of General Demographic Characteristics California* (U.S. Census Bureau online: 2001). The fact that the rate of increase in California incomes was below the national average during the time when California housing prices skyrocketed is from page 238 of a 1995 book by William A. Fischel titled *Regulatory Takings: Law, Economics, and Politics*. [Land use restrictions in Loudoun County, Virginia, were described in the *Washington Post* of July 24, 2001, in a story beginning on page B1, titled "Loudoun Adopts Strict Controls on Development" by Michael Laris. The fact that nearly half the rent-controlled apartments in San Francisco had only one tenant is from page 21 of *San Francisco Housing DataBook*, a 2001 study commissioned by the city and produced by consultants called Bay Area Economics. The fact that Urban Renewal destroyed more housing than it created and that more than three-fifths of the people displaced by Urban Renewal were black or Puerto Rican can be found on pages 6–7 and 221 of *The Federal Bulldozer* (1964 edition) by Martin Anderson. Jacob Riis' observations on the frugality of Jews living in the slums on the lower side of New York are from pages 71–72 and 84 of *How The Other Half Lives*, 1970 edition, published by The Harvard University Press. The fact that most Jewish immigrants came to the United States with their fares prepaid by family members already living in

America is from pages 112–113 of "Immigration of Russian Jews to the United States: Background and Structure" by Simon Kuznets in *Perspectives in American History*, Vol. IX (1973). Among the Irish immigrants, as well, at least one-third, "and possibly as many as one half," crossed the Atlantic with their fares paid by family members already living in America, according to page 394 of "The Irish Famine Emigration to the United States," in *Perspectives in American History*, Vol. X (1976). Overcrowding on the lower east side of New York when it was a predominantly Jewish neighborhood was discussed in an article in the September, 13, 1966 issue of the *New York Times Magazine* titled "The Negro Today is Like the Immigrant Yesterday," by Irving Kristol. Improvements in the housing of Southern blacks in the nineteenth century are discussed on pages 108–109, 111 of *Competition and Coercion* by Robert Higgs. Discussions of black Philadelphians in the nineteenth century are from pages 7, 34–35, 316 of *The Philadelphia Negro* by W. E. B. DuBois. The lesser amount of racial segregation in nineteenth century Northern cities, compared to their twentieth century ghettos, is mentioned in a footnote on page 176 of a 1970 book by St. Clair Drake and Horace B. Cayton titled *Black Metropolis*; in Chapter 1 of *Black Chicago* by Allan H. Spear; on pages 26, 55, 69, and 73 of *Before the Ghetto* by David M. Katzman; on page 12 of *Harlem: The Making of a Ghetto* by Gilbert Osofsky; on page 7 of *The Philadelphia Negro* by W. E. B. DuBois; and on page 127 of *The Secret City* by Constance Green. Official government policies promoting racial segregation are discussed on pages 24–25 of a 1978 book titled *The Builders* by Martin Mayer. Data on the continuing segregation of the descendants of northern and southern Europeans in the United States are from page 154 of *Affirmative Discrimination* by Nathan Glazer. Examples of improving race relations in Northern cities in the nineteenth century are cited, along with the sources, on pages 70 and 71 of my *Markets and Minorities*—and the subsequent retrogressions in race relations in the North on pages 72 and 73. Hostile reactions to Southern migrants within the existing black communities in Northern cities have been documented in many places, including pages 66–67 and pages 73–76 of the first volume of *Black Metropolis* by Drake and Cayton; page 168 of *Black Chicago* by Allen Spear; pages 284–285 of the 1971 edition of *The Negro in the United States* by E. Franklin Frazier; pages 96–97 of *Black Migration: Movement North,*

1900–1920 by Florette Henri; page 44 of *Harlem: The Making of a Ghetto* by Gilbert Ososky; and in Figure 1 (after page 100) of *Ethnic Enterprise in America* by Ivan H. Light. The spread of cholera through nineteenth century Irish neighborhoods was discussed on page 114 of *Boston's Immigrants* by Oscar Handlin and page 181 of *To the Golden Door* by George Potter. Violence in Irish neighborhoods in various cities is discussed on page 238 of *To the Golden Door* by George Potter p. 238; on page 126 of *Immigrant Milwaukee, 1836–1860* by Kathleen Neils Conzen; and on page 30 of *The Irish in America* by Carl Wittke.

CHAPTER 5: RISKY BUSINESS

Information on low-income residents doing their shopping and banking in higher-income neighborhoods is from pages 10 and 28 of *The Thin Red Line: How the Poor Still Pay More*, written by David Dante Trout and published in San Francisco in 1993 by the Western Regional Office of Consumers Union. The subtitle refers to an earlier study, *The Poor Pay More* by Theodore Caplovitz. Neither study explains the systemic economic causes behind the things they describe but this was done by economics professor Walter E. Williams in an article titled "Why the Poor Pay More: An Alternative Explanation" which appeared in *Social Science Quarterly* in September 1973, pages 372–379. The problems encountered by banks lending in "subprime" markets were reported in the *Wall Street Journal* of August 16, 2001 in a front-page story titled "As Economy Slows, 'Subprime' Lending Looks Even Riskier." The Federal Housing Authority's higher delinquency rates on loans to lower income buyers from page 19 of the November 18–24, 2002 issue of *The Washington Post National Weekly Edition* under the title "A Day Late, a Dollar Short," by Caroline E. Mayer.

Ralph Nader's comments about automobile safety are from his book *Unsafe at Any Speed*, pages vii, ix, x, 14, 18, 26, 42. Automobile fatality rates are from pages 719 and 720 of the U. S. Bureau of the Census's 1975 publication *Historical Statistics of the United States: Colonial Times to 1970*. The results of the government study of the safety of the Corvair were reported in the *Congressional Record: Senate*, March 27, 1973, pages 9748 to 9774. Its conclusion about the Corvair's performance is quoted from the

Wall Street Journal of July 23, 1971 (on-line) in an article by Charles B. Camp titled, "Popularity of Nader Declines to Its Nadir Among Corvair Owners." Information on New Jersey's experience under state regulation of automobile insurance is from page 24 of *The Economics of Life* by Gary Becker and Guity Nashat Becker. The quote from the Japanese pilot about the risks of wearing parachutes in aerial combat are from page 123 of *Samurai* by Saburo Sakai, 1963 edition published by Ballantine Books. The quote about re-insurance from the London magazine, *The Economist* is from its June 30, 2001 issue, page 66, in an article titled "Filling A Gap." Information on the Swiss Reinsurance Company is from *An Introduction to Reinsurance*, a brochure published by Swiss Re. Information on varying motor vehicle death rates by age are from page 109 of *The Insurance Information Institute Fact Book 2001*. Per capita agricultural output and meat consumption in the Soviet Union were discussed on page 61 of *The Turning Point* by Nikolai Shmelev and Vladimir Popov. The comment on higher death rates from natural disasters in poorer countries were made in an article by Indian economist Batrun S. Mitra titled "Dealing with Natural Disasters: Role of the Market" in the December 2000 issue of *Journal des Economistes et des Etudes Humaine*. The quotation from Paul Samuelson in defense of social insurance schemes and the economic and demographic data on their problems are from an article titled "Snares and Delusions" on pages 5 and 6 of a special section within the February 16, 2002 issue of *The Economist*. The special section is titled "Time to Grow Up."

CHAPTER 6: THE ECONOMICS OF DISCRIMINATION

Discrimination against black workers in public utilities was reported on page 96 of *Negro Employment in Public Utilities* by Bernard E. Anderson, published by the University of Pennsylvania Press in 1970. W. E. B. DuBois' comments on the hiring of black workers in the nineteenth century are from pages 323 and 395 of *The Philadelphia Negro*. Bias against lower-caste people in India is discussed on page 553 of *Competing Equalities* by Marc Galanter. The comment that the Chinese could do everything better and more cheaply than Malays is from page 25 of *The Malay Dilemma* by

Mahatir bin Mohamad, published in Kuala Lumper by Federal Publications in 1983. The comment about the more "thrusting" people of southern Nigeria was quoted on page 178 of *Ethnic Groups in Conflict* by Donald L. Horowitz. Similar comments from various other countries are quoted on pages 171 to 181 of the same book. The quoted paragraph about Japanese immigrants by an advocate of restricting their immigration was quoted on page 123 of *East to America: A History of the Japanese in the United States* by Robert A. Wilson and Bill Hosokawa. Pre-World War II discrimination against blacks and Jews by non-profit organizations is discussed on pages 695 and 705 of "Through the Back Door, Academic Racism and the Negro Scholar" by Michael R. Winston in the Summer 1971 issue of *Daedalus*; on page 480 of *American Democracy* by Harold J. Laski, and on page 323 of *An American Dilemma* by Gunnar Myrdal. Violations of apartheid laws by white employers are discussed on page 164 of *Apartheid: A History* by Brian Lapping and page 41 of *Capitalism and Apartheid* by Merle Lipton. Expansion of Jewish ghettoes during the Thirty Years' War is discussed in Chapter V of *European Jewry in the Age of Mercantilism: 1550–1750* by Jonathan I. Israel. The relationship between the Jews and the Poles in Chicago in the early twentieth century is discussed on page 229 of *The Ghetto* by Lewis Wirth. The fact that black young men from homes with newspapers, magazines, and library cards had the same incomes as white young men of the same description when they had the same education is from Chapter 4 *Black Elites* by Richard Freeman. The similarity of blacks, whites, and Hispanics of the same age with the same IQs is reported on page 323 of *The Bell Curve* by Richard J. Herrnstein and Charles Murray. The fact that single women who had worked continuously into their thirties had slightly higher incomes than single men of the same description is from page 203 of *The Economic Report of the President, 1973*. The non-comparability of untouchable and caste Hindu students who seemed at first to be comparable is from pages 357, 366, 391, 396, 406, 414, and 418 of a doctoral dissertation at the Tata Institute of Social Science in Bombay (Mumbai) 1982 titled "Inequality in Higher Education: A Study of Scheduled Caste Students in Medical Colleges of Bombay by Padma RamKrishna Velaskar. The non-comparability of black and white faculty members in the United States is from pages 81 to 89

of a study of mine titled "Affirmative Action in Faculty Hiring," reprinted
in *Education: Assumptions versus History*. Qualitative differences between
students from different social groups in Malaysia, Israel, Sri Lanka, India,
and the United States are documented in the following studies: Mohamed
Suffian bin Hashim, "Problems and Issues of Higher Education Develop-
ment in Malaysia," *Development of Higher Education in Southeast Asia: Prob-
lems and Issues* (Singapore: Regional Institute of Higher Education and
Development, 1973), pp. 56–78; Chandra Richard de Silva, "Sinhala-Tamil
Relations and Education in Sri Lanka: The University Admissions Issue—
The First Phase, 1971–7," *From Independence to Statehood: Managing Ethnic
Conflict in Five African and Asian States*, edited by R. B. Goldmann and A. J.
Wilson (London: Frances Pinter, 1984), pp. 125–146; Sammy Smooha and
Yochanan Peres, "The Dynamics of Ethnic Equality: the Case of Israel,"
Studies of Israeli Society, edited by Ernest Krausz, (New Brunswick: Transac-
tion Books, 1980), p. 173; Suma Chitnis, "Positive Discrimination in India
With Reference to Education," *From Independence to Statehood*, pp. 31–43;
Thomas Sowell, "Ethnicity in A Changing America," *Daedalus*, Winter
1978, pp. 231–232. The study claiming racial discrimination in mortgage
lending was reported in many places, including the front page of the *Washington Post* of June 6, 1993 under the title, "A Pattern of Bias in Mortgage
Loans" by Joel Glenn Brenner and on page A1 of the March 31, 1992 issue
of the *Wall Street Journal* in a story titled "Behind the Figures: Federal Reserve Detail Pervasive Racial Gap in Mortgage Lending," by Paulette
Thomas. The fact that whites were turned down for mortgage loans more
often than Asians was reported on page A8 of the November 30, 1992 issue
of *The Wall Street Journal* in a story titled "Blacks Can Face a Host of Trying
Conditions in Getting Mortgages," by Paulette Thomas. The differing qualifications of black and other mortgage loan applicants is discussed in Chapter 15 of *Backfire* by Bob Zelnick. The attribution of residual differences in
mortgage loan approval rates was attributed to discrimination by Alicia H.
Munnell in *Mortgage Lending in Boston: Interpreting HMDA Data*, Working
Paper No. 92–7, October 1992, Federal Reserve Bank of Boston, pages 2, 24,
25. Differences in wealth by blacks and whites in the same income brackets
are shown on page 20 of the Census Bureau publication *Current Population*

Reports, Series P–23, No. 173. Documented details on the many ways that women and men with the "same" education differ can be found on pages 38–40 of my *The Vision of the Anointed*. The great over-representation of people of German ancestry in the St. Petersburg Academy of Science is discussed on page 195 of *The Volga Germans* by Fred C. Koch; the over-representation of Jews among physicians in Poland and Hungary between the two World Wars is discussed on page 339 of *Diaspora* by Howard M. Sachar and on page 27 of *The Jews of East Central Europe between the World Wars* by Ezra Mendelsohn; and the over-representation of southern Nigerians in the professions in northern Nigeria was discussed on pages 40 and 41 of Nigeria's *Statistical Yearbook 1965*, published by the Ministry of Economic Planning in Kaduna. The statement by an Illinois state official condemning the use of tests that were harder to "disadvantaged" minorities to pass is quoted from pages 3133 and 3134 of a compendium compiled by the U. S. Equal Employment Opportunity Commission under the title, *Legislative History of Titles VII and XI of Civil Rights Act of 1964*.

CHAPTER 7: THE ECONOMIC
DEVELOPMENT OF NATIONS

The epigraph at the beginning of the chapter is from page 79 of *From Subsistence to Exchange and Other Essays* by Peter Bauer, published in 2000 by Princeton University Press. Comparisons between Argentina's economic standing in the world in the early twentieth century and in the early twenty-first century are from page 26 of *The Economist* of March 2, 2002, under the title, "A Decline Without Parallel." Changes in the relative positions of India and China were reported on page 28 of a study conducted by McKinsey consultants titled "India—From Emerging to Surging." The information that the United States, with less than 5 percent of the world's population, produces more than 30 percent of the world's output is from page 4 of a special section titled "Present at the Creation" in *The Economist* of June 29, 2002. The tenuousness of property rights in many Third World countries was discovered in an international study reported in *The Mystery of Capital* by Peruvian economist Hernando de Soto, published in 2000 by

Basic Books. The lengthy processes required to get legal title to real estate in Egypt and Haiti are from page 20 to 21 of that book. The illegal buses, taxis and food vendors in Third World countries are discussed on page 28. The enormous value of legally unrecognized economic assets in various poor countries is discussed on page 32 to 35. The role of property rights in enabling strangers to combine their assets for corporate ventures beyond the reach of any given individual is discussed on pages 56 and 61. Another analysis of the same phenomenon appeared in *The Economist* of March 31, 2001 under the title "Poverty and Property Rights," pages 20 to 22. The greater accessibility of San Francisco from China than from the banks of the Missouri was mentioned on page 65 of *The Chinese of America* by Jack Chen, published by Harper & Row in 1980. The importation of kerosene by the city of Tiflis from Texas was discussed on page 60 of *The Prize: The Epic Quest for Oil, Money, and Power,* by Daniel Yergin, published by Simon & Schuster in 1990. Similarly huge disparities in costs between land transport and water transport in Africa, Japan, and England are mentioned on page 5 of *The Geography of Modern Africa* by William A. Hance, published by Columbia University Press in 1964; page 515 of *East Asia: Tradition & Transformation*, revised edition, by John K. Fairbank, Edwin O. Reischauer, and Albert M. Craig, published by Houghton Mifflin Co. in 1989; and on page 72 of "Coal and Steam Power," by Nick von Tunzelmann in *Atlas of Industrializing Britain 1790–1914* published by Methuen & Co., Ltd., in 1986. The cost of shipping wheat in the Ottoman Empire is from page 184 of "Imperial Borderlands or Capitalist Periphery? Redefining Balkan Backwardness," by John R. Lampe, in *The Origins of Backwardness in Eastern Europe*, edited by Daniel Chirot. The relative costs of shipping oil by various modes is from page 124 of Walker Connor, *Ethnonationalism: The Quest for Understanding* by Walker Connor, published by Princeton University Press in 1994. Samarkand's role as a crossroads of desert routes is mentioned on pages 176 and 178 of *Before European* by Janet L. Abu-Lughod. The manpower used to carry cocoa by porters and by train is discussed on page 54 of *The Economic Revolution in British West Africa* by Allan McPhee published by Frank Cass & Co., Ltd., 1971. The fact that every one of the early industrial regions in Europe had the benefit of navigable waterways was discussed on pages 492–593 of *An Historical Geography of Europe: 1800–1914* by N. J. G. Pounds, published by Cambridge University Press. The lack of fossil fuels, urbanization, railroads, and rivers in the Balkans, and its cultural fracturing, are mentioned on pages 43, 132, 178–179, 430, 459, and 485 of the same book. The characterization of the Balkans as "self-sufficient" is from page 488 of the same work. The locations of Russian rivers are discussed on page 2 of *The Industrialization of Russia: A Historical Perspective*, third edition, by William L. Blackwell, published by Arlington Heights, Illinois: Harland Davidson in 1994. The role of waterways in Genoa and Mombasa as sole outlets for productive regions was discussed on pages 263 and 283 of *Influences of Geographic Environment* by Ellen Churchill Semple, published by Henry Holt and Co. in 1911. On the role of the port of Dubrovnik, see page 147 of "The Geographical Setting of Medieval Dubrovnik," by Josip Roglic in *Geographical Essays on Eastern Europe*, edited by Norman J. G. Pounds, published by Indiana University. The role of the Gulf stream in Europe's weather is discussed on pages 14, 92 of *Europe: A Geographical Survey of the Continent* by Roy E. H. Mellor and E. Alistair Smith, published by Columbia University Press in 1979. The dearth of rain in Spain is mentioned on page 365 of *An Economic History of Spain* by James Vicens Vives, published by Princeton University Press in 1969 and the dearth of rainfall in Sicily is mentioned on page 35 of *The Sting of Change: Sicilians in Sicily and Australia* by Constance Cronin, published by the University of Chicago Press in 1970. The incomes of immigrants from Southern and Eastern Europe in the United States are discussed on page 15 of U. S. Commission on Civil Rights, *The Economic Status of Americans of Southern and Eastern European Ancestry*, published by the U. S. Commission on Civil Rights in 1986. These immigrants also took more years to reach the average income of native-born Americans. See Barry R. Chiswick, "The Economic Progress of Immigrants: Some Apparently Universal Patterns," *The Gateway: U. S. Immigration Issues and Policies* (Washington: The American Enterprise Institute, 1982), page 147. Illiteracy among these immigrants is discussed on page 72 of *Ethnic Patterns in American Cities* by Stanley Lieberson, published by the Free Press of Glencoe in 1963. The lag of their children in education and IQ are discussed in

Peter Fox, *The Poles in America* (New York: Arno Press, 1970), p. 96; Leonard P. Ayres, *Laggards in Our Schools: A Study of Retardation and Elimination in City School Systems* (New York: Russell Sage Foundation, 1909), pp. 107–108; *Reports of the Immigration Commission*, 61st Congress, 3rd Session, Vol. I: *The Children of Immigrants in Schools* (Washington: Government Printing Office, 1911), p. 48–49, 89, 90; Thomas Sowell, "Race and I.Q. Reconsidered," *Essays and Data on American Ethnic Groups*, edited by Thomas Sowell (Washington: The Urban Institute, 1978), p. 207. That many Southern Europeans tended to speak local dialects, rather than the official languages of their respective countries was discussed on page 58 of *Southern Europeans in Australia* by Charles A. Price, published by the Australian National University, 1979), p. 58. Their geographic origins are mentioned on pages 16, 17n, and 24 of the same book. The earnings and occupations of various Southern European groups in Australia are discussed on pages 47, 63, and 68 of *A Profile of the Italian Community in Australia*, by Helen Ware, published by the Australian Institute of Multicultural Affairs in 1981. Differences in rainfall on different sides of mountain ranges are discussed on page 31 of *The Mountains of the Mediterranean* by J. R. McNeill and on page 132 to 133 of *Physical Geography of the Global Environment* by H. J. de Blij and Peter O. Mueller, published by John Wiley & Sons, Inc. The ratio of people to land in India is from page 72 of *Asian Drama* by Gunnar Myrdal, abridged edition, published in 1972 by Vintage Press. The fact that Germans ate dogs and cats to avoid starvation during the blockade in the First World War is mentioned on page 79 of *Against the Dead Hand: The Uncertain Struggle for Global Capitalism* by Brink Lindsey. The classic study of Stalin's man-made famine in the Soviet Union is *Harvest of Sorrow* by Robert Conquest. Horrifying as Dr. Conquest's estimate—in the millions—of the deaths during this famine were, when the Soviet archives were eventually opened in the last years of the Soviet Union, it turned out that he had under-estimated how many had died.

INDEX